AN INTEGRATED THEORY OF
LINGUISTIC DESCRIPTIONS

AN INTEGRATED THEORY OF LINGUISTIC DESCRIPTIONS

JERROLD J. KATZ
PAUL M. POSTAL

RESEARCH MONOGRAPH NO. 26
THE M.I.T. PRESS, CAMBRIDGE, MASSACHUSETTS

ACKNOWLEDGMENT

This is Special Technical Report Number 9 of the Research
Laboratory of Electronics of the Massachusetts Institute of
Technology.

The Research Laboratory of Electronics is an interdepart-
mental laboratory in which faculty members and graduate stu-
dents from numerous academic departments conduct research.

The research reported in this document was made possible
in part by support extended the Massachusetts Institute of
Technology, Research Laboratory of Electronics, jointly by
the U.S. Army (Electronics Materiel Agency), the U.S. Navy
(Office of Naval Research), and the U.S. Air Force (Office of
Scientific Research) under Contract DA36-039-AMC-03200(E);
and in part by Grant DA-SIG-36-039-61-G14; additional support
was received from the U.S. Air Force (Electronic Systems
Division) under Contract AF 19(628)-2487; the National Science
Foundation (Grant G-16526); the National Institutes of Health
(Grant MH-04737-03); and the National Aeronautics and Space
Administration (Grant NsG-496).

Second Printing, December 1965
Third Printing, May 1967

Library of Congress Catalog Card Number: 64-17356

Printed in the United States of America

To the memory of my father

Isadore Katz

and

to my father and mother

Bernard and Margaret Postal

FOREWORD

There has long been a need in science and engineering for systematic publication of research studies larger in scope than a journal article but less ambitious than a finished book. Much valuable work of this kind is now published only in a semiprivate way, perhaps as a laboratory report, and so may not find its proper place in the literature of the field. The present contribution is the twenty-sixth of the M.I.T. Press Research Monographs, which we hope will make selected timely and important research studies readily accessible to libraries and to the independent worker.

J. A. Stratton

PREFACE

In any linguistic study, it is necessary to distinguish sharply between language and speech. Although this distinction has been classic in linguistics at least since the time of F. de Saussure, modern linguistics, influenced by behavioristic and positivistic ideas, has often confused the two. Because of this confusion, the importance of this classic distinction must be re-emphasized.

A language is a system of abstract objects analogous in significant respects to such a cultural object as a symphony. Speech is the actual verbal behavior that manifests the linguistic competence of one who has learned the appropriate system of abstract objects. Thus speech is analogous to the performances of a symphony in just the sense in which the language is analogous to the symphony itself. But just as symphonic performances are not invariant realizations of a symphony, so speech performances are not invariant realizations of the abstract objects that comprise the language. In both cases, besides the competence of performers who have learned the appropriate abstract objects, many other parameters partially determine the character of actual performances, among which are the skills and abilities of the performers, the context of the performance, and the character of the audience.

In the widest sense, linguistics is concerned with both language and speech. But a scientific understanding of speech can be gained only on the basis of extensive knowledge about language. For this reason, linguists have traditionally narrowed the scope of their investigations to the study of language proper. In this study, linguists pursue two interrelated goals. First, they seek to construct descriptions of particular natural languages. A description of a natural language is a scientific theory in the form of a system of rules from which the phonological, syntactic, and semantic facts about the language may be derived as consequences. Second, linguists seek to construct a theory of the nature of language. Such a theory should represent the structure common to all natural languages in a model that explains why the rules in the descriptions of particular natural languages have the form they do and which of the concepts used in these rules are linguistic universals. This theory receives support from empirically successful descriptions of particular natural languages: the theory is justified to the extent that the rules of every correct description have the form prescribed by the theory, and every correct description employs the concepts to which the theory accords the status of linguistic universals.

The present monograph is intended as a contribution to a theory of the nature of language. Its major aim is to provide an adequate means of incorporating the grammatical and the semantic descriptions of a language into one integrated description. The conception of a <u>linguistic description</u> proposed here combines the generative conception of grammar developed by Chomsky with the conception of semantics proposed by Katz and Fodor. We argue that our conception achieves an integration of these conceptions of grammar and semantics leading to significant answers to certain outstanding questions about the nature of syntactic and semantic descriptions of particular natural languages. Among the questions for which definite answers are given are these: What are the syntactic structures that are semantically interpreted in describing the meaning of a sentence? Do transformations contribute anything to the meaning of sentences? What changes in the form of a syntactic description must be made to accord with this integration of syntactic and semantic descriptions? In this monograph we justify both our proposal for integrating these phases of linguistic description and the answers to the above questions, which follow from our proposal. We show that the sort of linguistic descriptions to which our proposal leads provide the best systematization of the grammatical and semantic facts of English.

No index appears in this monograph because the nature of the material makes one unnecessary.

We wish to take this opportunity to express our gratitude to those who helped us. We thank Noam Chomsky for his interest and encouragement as well as for many valuable suggestions, which have been incorporated into the final version. We are also grateful to those of our friends and colleagues whose comments have added both to the content and clarity of this monograph. We thank those members of the staff of the Research Laboratory of Electronics who assisted us at various stages in the preparation of the manuscript.

Cambridge, Massachusetts   Jerrold J. Katz
April 1964   Paul M. Postal

CONTENTS

Chapter 1

INTRODUCTION

A linguistic description of a natural language is an attempt to
reveal the nature of a fluent speaker's mastery of that language.
This mastery is manifested in the speaker's ability to communicate with other speakers of the language: to produce appropriate
sentences that convey information, ask questions, give commands,
etc., and to understand the sentences of other speakers. Thus
a linguistic description must reconstruct the principles underlying the ability of speakers to communicate with one another. Such
a reconstruction is a scientific theory whose statements represent the linguistic structure characteristic of the language and
whose deductive consequences enable the linguist to explain sentence use and comprehension[1] in terms of features of this structure.

The present study seeks to develop an integrated conception
of the nature of a linguistic description of a natural language. It
builds on work accomplished within the framework of generative
grammar, but extends that work by bringing it in line with recent developments in semantics. According to this conception,
a linguistic description of a natural language consists of three
components: syntactic, semantic, and phonological.[2] The syntactic component is fundamental in the sense that the other two
components both operate on its output. That is, the syntactic
component is the generative source in the linguistic description.
This component generates the abstract formal structures underlying actual sentences. These structures consist of a string of
the minimal syntactically functioning elements (formatives) together with a structural description specifying the syntactic properties of the string. The other components of a linguistic description provide each of these generated formal structures with a
semantic interpretation and a phonological representation. The
semantic interpretation of a particular syntactic structure describes the meaning of the sentence which that structure underlies. The phonological representation assigned to a structure
generated by the syntactic component includes a phonetic representation of that structure which serves as the input to the mechanism of speech production. This input imposes a set of necessary and sufficient conditions on the output of this mechanism.
If this set of conditions is satisfied, the output of the mechanism

1

of speech production is a physical event which is a realization in sound of the sentence represented by the formal syntactic structure.[3]

In such a tripartite theory of linguistic descriptions, certain psychological claims are made about the speaker's capacity to communicate fluently. The fundamental claim is that the fluent speaker's ability to use and understand speech involves a basic mechanism that enables him to construct the formal syntactic structures underlying the sentences which these utterances represent, and two subsidiary mechanisms: one that associates a set of meanings with each formal syntactic structure and another that maps such structures into phonetic representations, which are, in turn, the input to his speech apparatus.

Each of the three components of a linguistic description is a functionally interdependent part of the conceptual machinery of a single, integrated theory.[4] The general theory of linguistic descriptions — the theory seeking to specify the common features of all empirically successful individual linguistic descriptions — must state these functional interconnections in order to characterize the notion 'linguistic description'. The connections between the syntactic and phonological components are described in some recent and forthcoming works[5] and will not concern us here. On the other hand, there are no theoretically significant relations between the semantic and phonological components, since these components perform independent operations on quite different features of the structures generated by the syntactic component. This characteristic of linguistic descriptions is the formal analogue of Saussure's dictum that the connection between form and meaning is arbitrary. Moreover, the arbitrariness of this connection can be explained in terms of the fact that the semantic and phonological components perform independent operations on different features of the syntactic output. We shall explain in greater detail how this is so after we develop the necessary conceptual machinery.

The relations between the syntactic and semantic components have not been explicated until recently because there has been no framework within which to construct such an explication. Although these relations are of the utmost theoretical significance, there has not been a clear conception of the internal structure of the semantic component upon which to base an account of the relations between the syntactic and semantic components. Thus decisions concerning the justification of the internal structure of one of these components could reasonably be made only in terms of considerations drawn exclusively from the sphere of that component. Arguments based upon semantic considerations that were offered in order to establish something about the syntactic component were justifiably regarded with extreme suspicion

because the semantic considerations themselves were too vague
to provide the necessary support. On the other hand, although
syntactic considerations were sufficiently clear and well understood to justify a treatment of a semantic question, the semantic
questions themselves were too confused to permit the formulation of answers explicit enough to be justified by clear-cut syntactic considerations.

This question of intercomponential justification is completely
independent of the long classic controversy about whether the
constructions defining syntactic concepts must contain some semantic features, i.e., the controversy about whether some of
the primitive terms of syntactic theory are semantic terms.[6]
This controversy has been further confused by the introduction
of the problem of whether an adequate discovery procedure for
syntactic components must employ semantic considerations. The
question of justification with which we are concerned is independent of this problem too.

The situation in which the relations between the syntactic and
semantic components are inexplicable has, we think, fundamentally changed now that there is an explicit proposal concerning the
internal structure of the semantic component, namely that made
in "The Structure of a Semantic Theory."[7] Given the specific
conception of the relations between the syntactic and semantic
components embodied in this proposal, one can go beyond the
purely internal point of view on matters of justification and make
decisions about the internal structure of one component based on
arguments in which considerations from the sphere of the other
component play a significant justificatory role.

This possibility allows one in principle to assess the adequacy
of a full linguistic description in terms of its over-all simplicity
and explanatory power. It is necessary to judge adequacy in this
holistic manner because by doing so the possibility of improving
one or two of the components at the expense of the other(s) is
eliminated. Certainly, it is methodologically unsound to improve
one or two of the components if such 'improvement' necessitates
constructing the other component(s) in a way that makes them incapable of accounting adequately for their phases of the speaker's
linguistic ability. For only the over-all linguistic description
is really an explanation of the speaker's linguistic abilities. And
if even one of the components fails, the whole linguistic description must fail as such an explanation.

Since there is now a sufficiently clear conception of the semantic component so that the requirement of maximum explanatory power and simplicity of the over-all linguistic description
can be utilized to determine the character of both the syntactic
and semantic components, we hope to accomplish two objectives.
The first is to exploit this requirement to extend and somewhat

revise the conception of the semantic component originally presented in "The Structure of a Semantic Theory." The second is to explore the ramifications that these extensions and revisions have for the internal structure of the syntactic component. If successful in these aims, we shall have provided a more comprehensive and integrated conception of the nature of a linguistic description, a conception in which the role of the semantic component and its relations to the other components are explicitly characterized.[8]

NOTES

1. We exclude aspects of sentence use and comprehension that are not explicable through the postulation of a generative mechanism as the reconstruction of the speaker's ability to produce and understand sentences. In other words, we exclude conceptual features such as the physical and sociological settings of utterances, attitudes, and beliefs of the speaker and hearer, perceptual and memory limitations, noise level of the settings, etc. For a discussion of these matters, cf. Katz and Fodor (1963).

2. We assume that each of these components contains a theory of deviation from well-formedness for their level of linguistic structure. Such theories should explain why some deviations are understood by speakers, while others are not, and should account for other facts of deviation as well. But we shall not be concerned here with this facet of a linguistic description. Cf. Chomsky (1964 a) and Katz (1964 a).

3. It is of course an oversimplification to identify a sentence with any utterance or set of utterances, since any real utterance has features that are not in any way determined by the linguistic system, i.e., not determined by the most detailed phonetic representation generated by the phonological component. These 'nonlinguistic' features include information about the speaker's identity, age, sex, emotional state, health, presence of food in the mouth, etc.

4. In the literature on generative grammar, the term 'grammar' has been used to refer to the syntactic and phonological components only. But this term has also had the sense of 'systematic theory of linguistic structure', chiefly because no formal treatment of semantics was envisaged. We use the term 'linguistic description' to take over this latter sense.

5. Halle (1959, 1962); Chomsky (1963, 1964 b); Halle and Chomsky (in preparation).

6. Cf. Chomsky (1955 b).

7. Katz and Fodor (1963).

8. Although the discussion in this study primarily concerns abstract questions about the nature of language, rather than questions about the description of specific natural languages, the examples upon which our answers to these questions are based are drawn almost exclusively from English. We have not overlooked the task of testing our theory against examples drawn from a wide variety of languages. However, we are here concerned more with the formulation and presentation of our theory than with its defense. Moreover, a full-scale empirical test of a theory such as ours is obviously not possible at the present time, because other languages have not received an extensive enough formal description for them to provide the kind of examples needed.

Chapter 2

THE SYNTACTIC AND SEMANTIC COMPONENTS

2.1 The Syntactic Component

The syntactic component of a linguistic description of a natural language must be a system of rules which enumerates the infinite set of abstract formal structures which underlie the sentences of the language. We assume that the correct form for this generative device is a transformational syntax in the sense described by Chomsky.[1] Such a system assigns to each string of formatives generated one or more <u>structural descriptions</u> (SD) in the form of a finite sequence of labeled bracketings — <u>phrase markers</u> (P-markers) — and a <u>transformational marker</u> (T-marker), which indicates the configurations of transformations applied in the derivation of the string of formatives.

A transformational syntactic component has two major parts containing fundamentally different kinds of rules. The initial or <u>phrase structure</u> subcomponent contains only rules which operate on strings of symbols. Each such rule operates on a fixed string by replacing a single, nonnull symbol by a fixed nonnull string distinct from (and not containing) the initial, rewritten symbol. For example, a much oversimplified set of phrase structure rules might be the following:

    a. Sentence → Noun Phrase + Verb Phrase
    b. Noun Phrase → John
    c. Noun Phrase → truth
    d. Verb Phrase → Verb + Noun Phrase
    e. Verb → love + s

Such rules permit the construction of <u>derivations</u>: finite sequences of strings of symbols, beginning with the initial sequence of the grammar # Sentence # (where # is the symbol for sentence boundary), and with each successive line formed by the application of one rule to one symbol in a string. One of the derivations produced by the above rules consists of the sequence (boundaries omitted): [Sentence, Noun Phrase + Verb Phrase, John + Verb Phrase, John + Verb + Noun Phrase, John + love + s + Noun Phrase, John + love + s + truth]. There is an algorithm or mechanical procedure for associating a labeled bracketing or P-marker with each such derivation. With this derivation, for example, we can associate the P-marker shown in Diagram 2.1.

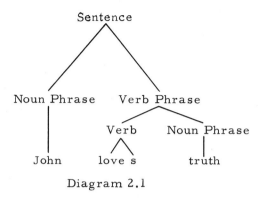

Diagram 2.1

Such labeled bracketings formally render the notions of grammatical category, part of speech, or immediate constituent structure. In the last lines of derivations each substring of symbols
that is uniquely traceable back to some node labeled X in a P-
marker can be said to be a (member of the category or constituent) X'. For example, in Diagram 2.1, John is a Noun Phrase;
love + s + truth is a Verb Phrase. If a string B is an X, X is said
to dominate B. Then X immediately dominates the string B if
there are no constituents C, D, etc., such that X dominates C
+ D + etc. where C + D + etc. dominates B. The output of the
phrase structure subpart of the syntactic component is then a
finite set of such P-markers, each describing the constituency
relations between the morphemes that are its terminal elements.[2]
   The rules of the transformational subpart of the syntactic component operate on the P-markers produced by the phrase structure component, and derive new P-markers. It is crucial to distinguish between those P-markers in an SD which are derived
exclusively by phrase structure rules and those whose derivation
involves one or more transformational rules. The former type
will be referred to as underlying P-markers. The latter are
called derived P-markers. The terminal symbols of underlying
P-markers are referred to as morphemes. We can illustrate
these ideas as follows. Diagram 2.2 is the underlying P-marker
of

(1) does John sleep

while Diagram 2.3 represents one of its derived P-markers, in
fact the last such: that produced by the last transformation in the
T-marker of (1).[3] The symbol for word and sentence boundary
is #. It should be emphasized that derived P-markers are a
function of the underlying P-markers of the sentences to which
they are assigned and the T-markers associated with these sen-

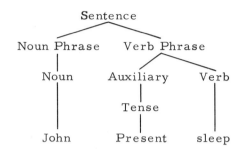

Diagram 2.2

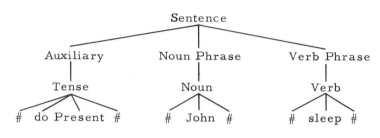

Diagram 2.3

tences but nothing else. Derived P-markers are thus 'predict-
able' and contain no independent information. Among the derived
P-markers for any sentence is the last one, which is the result
of application of all the transformations in that sentence's T-
marker. This is referred to as the final derived P-marker. The
elements of its last line are then formatives in the sense of our
introductory discussion. Final derived P-markers thus represent the actual strings of formatives (in the correct order) of
which sentences consist. At this level, sentences are also bracketed into nonoverlapping words so that final derived P-markers
also represent the actual strings of words of which sentences
consist. Hence, such P-markers represent the most superficial
aspect of hierarchical categorization. Diagram 2.3 is a final
derived P-marker.

The set of morphemes for a language is not necessarily identical with the set of formatives (because transformations may add
or delete terminal symbols), and in fact it almost certainly never
is. For example, in English do as a part of auxiliaries is a formative and thus present in final derived P-markers like Diagram
2.2 but is not a morpheme and thus not present in underlying P-
markers. Similarly, in all languages word boundaries probably
are formatives but not morphemes.

The rules of the phrase structure subcomponent serve to map
strings of symbols into other strings of symbols, with the restriction that symbols may not be deleted or permuted. Such rules

have the important limitation that <u>they do not incorporate the</u>
<u>power of variable reference</u> in the following sense. When a sym-
bol A occurs in a phrase structure rule, A is not a variable having some particular set of strings of morphemes or fomatives
as its values. Rather, A refers to occurrences of the symbol
A in the lines of derivations. Thus, a phrase structure rule like
'A → B' is an instruction to replace any occurrence of the symbol A by an occurrence of the symbol B. And yet it is quite crucial in actual linguistic description that there be rules whose symbols can have actual strings of morphemes and formatives as
values. Thus, for example, such natural and simple rules as
'the verb agrees with the subject noun in gender and number' cannot be described in phrase structure terms for exactly this reason. Such an informal rule says that there is a certain set of
strings of symbols found on nouns, and in each case a verb that
co-occurs with a particular noun must have the same string as
the noun. Phrase structure rules can describe such situations,
which abound in natural languages, only with a separate rule for
each pair of agreeing sequences. The rules of the transformational component operate on P-markers and map these into new
P-markers. The power of variable reference in the sense described above is introduced by stating the domains of transformations in terms of a set of conditions on P-markers. Any P-marker or set of P-markers which meets these conditions falls into
the domain of the transformation. Thus, unlike a phrase structure rule that applies only to a set of strings all of which must
share some fixed subsequence, a transformation applies to a
set of strings that need share no subsequences whatever, but
need only have a fixed representation in terms of P-marker structure.

   This notion of the domain of a transformation can be made clearer by an example. The verbal agreement rule given earlier might
be stated as a transformation like

$$\text{Gender + Number, Noun Stem, Verb, } X \Longrightarrow 1, 2, 1 + 3, 4$$
$$\qquad\qquad 1 \qquad\qquad\qquad 2 \qquad 3 \quad 4$$

The numbered sequence of elements is called a <u>structure index</u>.
More generally, it is necessary to allow the domain of transformations to be stated by Boolean conditions on such simple sequences, and it is usual to extend the term 'structure index' to
cover these more complex characterizations. A structure index
defines the set of P-markers that may undergo the relevant transformation in the following way. Any terminal string (last line of
a P-marker) falls under the domain of the above rule if it can be
exhaustively broken up into four consecutive substrings such that
in its associated P-marker the first part <u>is a</u> (member of the

constituent or category sequence) Gender + Number, the second is a Noun Stem, the third is a Verb, and the fourth anything at all. Thus, Diagram 2.4 contains a P-marker which falls under this domain, but Diagrams 2.5 and 2.6 do not. The agreement transformation then operates, adding a duplicate of the first term of relevant P-markers to the left of the third term of these P-markers.

Transformational rules whose domains are so stated provide the power of variable reference since each structure index characterizes a wide set of different P-markers on which the transformations can operate. Thus the simple agreement transformation given above operates not only on P-markers like that in Diagram 2.4 but also on P-markers in which [Masculine] is replaced by [Feminine], [Singular] by [Plural], the Noun Stem [a] by any other noun stem, the constituent Adverb by any other postverbal constituent or null, etc. By including in its domain a single string of elements, a transformation characterizes a wide range of quite distinct strings upon which it may operate. These strings need only share a fixed structural property definable on P-markers. Hence, when elements like Noun Phrase, Verb Phrase, or other constituents or sequences of constituents appear in phrase structure rules, they refer to constant parts of strings; but when they occur in the structure indices of transformations, they are variables over sets of distinct parts of strings.

Besides a domain as stated above, each transformation contains a finite sequence of formal operations — elementary transformations. Each elementary transformation operates on n terms, where n is the number of terms in the structure index. These operations determine the changes to be made in the P-markers that fall in the transformation's domain. The different types of formal operation performed by elementary transformations — i. e., substitution, deletion, addition, permutation — jointly characterize the possible types of transformation. It is an important virtue of transformational grammars that the types of operation on strings possible in transformational derivations are much greater in variety than with phrase structure rules.

Given a particular P-marker, bracketed in a certain way in terms of a structure index, there must be a unique output P-marker, given the application of a particular elementary transformation. Thus each type of elementary transformation must have associated with it a particular condition stating how it affects P-markers to produce new P-markers. These principles of derived constituent structure must be stated in the general theory of linguistic descriptions. They are the analogue in the transformational part of the syntax of the algorithm which permits the construction of underlying P-markers from phrase structure rule derivations. The set of all elementary transformations

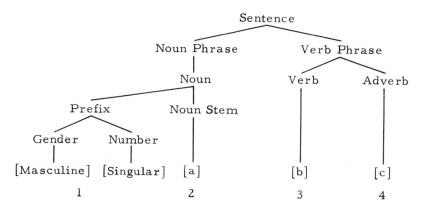

Diagram 2.4

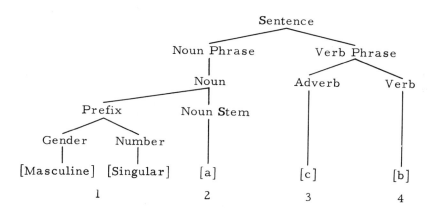

Diagram 2.5

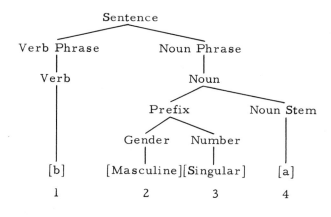

Diagram 2.6

and also their possible combinations in sequence are specified
in the general theory of linguistic descriptions. By fixing this
set precisely, one specifies, among other things, the maximum
number of terms upon which any transformation operates. This
accounts for our feeling that, for example, there is no rule of
natural language that permutes the first and seventy-ninth element in some string. In other words, rules can be stated with
relatively short domains.

The output of the phrase structure part of the syntactic component is a finite set of P-markers. But the output of the transformational part is an infinite set of (final derived) P-markers
plus associated T-markers.[4]   Thus the recursive mechanism
that accounts for the infinite properties of language lies within
the transformational subpart. More specifically, the recursive
power resides in generalized transformations, i.e., those which
operate on a set of P-markers (probably always two) to produce
a single new derived P-marker by embedding part or all of one
in the other or by conjoining the two in some way. Transformations which operate only on a single P-marker are referred to
as singulary. A sentence has more than one underlying P-marker just in case its T-marker contains at least one generalized
transformation. We shall have more to say about the singulary-
generalized distinction later, where it actually plays a role in
our discussions.[5]

2.2 The Semantic Component

As stated earlier, the semantic component of a linguistic description will be taken to be a projective device in the sense of
Katz and Fodor.[6]   Such a projective device consists of two parts:
first, a dictionary that provides a meaning for each of the lexical
items of the language, and second, a finite set of projection rules.
The projection rules of the semantic component assign a semantic interpretation to each string of formatives generated by the
syntactic component. The semantic interpretation that a string
of formatives has assigned to it provides a full analysis of its
cognitive meaning.

To obtain such semantic interpretations, each lexical item in
a string of formatives must receive a meaning on the basis of
the semantic information in the dictionary. The projection rules
then combine these meanings in a manner dictated by the syntactic description of the string to arrive at a characterization
of the meaning of the whole string and each of its constituents.
This process reconstructs the way in which a speaker is able
to obtain a meaning for a sentence from the meanings of its lexical items and its syntactic structure. Thus, the semantic component, if formulated correctly, provides an explanation of the
speaker's ability to determine the meaning of any sentence, in-

cluding ones wholly novel to him, as a compositional function of the antecedently known meanings of the lexical items in it.

Since some of the syntactic information represented in the SD of a sentence is required for the semantic component to assign that sentence a semantic interpretation, the input to the semantic component must be the output of the syntactic component. Thus the semantic component takes, one after the other, strings of formatives with their associated SD and operates on them to produce a semantic interpretation for each string. The first step in this operation is the assignment of the relevant semantic information from the dictionary to each lexical item in the string of formatives received from the syntactic component.

The entries in the dictionary must be in a normal form. This normal form must enable the dictionary to represent formally all the semantic information involved in the meaning of any lexical item. The conceptual apparatus of this normal form must be sufficient to represent every piece of semantic information required by the projection rules to assign correct semantic interpretations. An entry in this normal form for a lexical item must be a full analysis of the meaning of that lexical item: it must decompose the meaning of the lexical item into its most elementary components and state the semantic relations between them.

The normal form for a dictionary entry is as follows: an entry consists of a finite set of sequences of symbols, each sequence consisting of an initial subsequence of syntactic markers, followed by a subsequence of semantic markers, then, optionally, a distinguisher, and finally a selection restriction. Dictionary entries may be represented in the form of tree diagrams, like Diagram 2.7, where each sequence in the entry for the lexical item appears as a distinct path rooted at that lexical item.

Semantic markers are enclosed within parentheses, distinguishers within brackets, and selection restrictions within angles. The syntactic markers are unenclosed, and the dots in Diagram 2.7 indicate the possibility of further syntactic categorization, i. e. , into Animate Noun, Common Noun, Count Noun, etc. Each complete path — i.e. , each complete sequence of such symbols — represents a distinct sense of the lexical item in whose entry it appears. We shall refer to such paths as readings (of the lexical item). Thus a lexical item with n readings is represented as n-ways semantically ambiguous by its entry. In Diagram 2.7, for example, the lexical item bachelor is represented as four-ways semantically ambiguous, i. e. , as having four distinct senses.

Syntactic markers appearing in a dictionary entry differentiate senses of a lexical item which differ primarily in their 'part of speech' role — for example, the distinct senses of kill as a Verb and as a Noun.

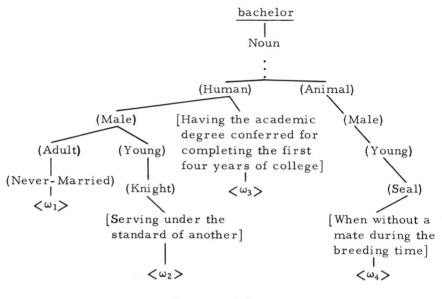

Diagram 2.7

Semantic markers are the formal elements that a semantic component uses to express general semantic properties. In contrast, distinguishers are the formal elements employed to represent what is idiosyncratic about the meaning of a lexical item. Thus, while a distinguisher differentiates a lexical item from those closest to it in meaning so that each distinguisher will be found only once in the dictionary, a semantic marker found in a reading of a certain lexical item will also be found in the readings of many other lexical items throughout the dictionary. The difference between semantic marker and distinguisher can be more fully appreciated by comparing the consequences of eliminating particular semantic markers and distinguishers from the dictionary. In the former case, the meaning given to very many lexical items by the dictionary would be altered and so would very many semantic relations between lexical items. However, in the latter case only a few distinctions in sense which were marked by the eliminated distinguisher would no longer be marked. This suggests that distinguishers may be regarded as semantic markers with maximally limited distribution in the dictionary.

The meaning of a lexical item is not an undifferentiated whole.[7] Rather, it is analyzable into atomic conceptual elements related to each other in certain ways. Semantic markers and distinguishers are intended as the symbolic devices which represent the atomic concepts out of which the sense of a lexical item is synthesized. Readings represent such synthesizations of atomic concepts.

A lexical item is ambiguous when it has more than one sense. Ambiguity at the lexical level is the source of semantic ambiguity at the sentence level. Thus, a necessary but not sufficient condition for a syntactically unambiguous sentence to be semantically ambiguous is that it contain at least one ambiguous lexical item. For example, the source of the semantic ambiguity in the sentence

(2) he enjoys wearing a light suit in the summer

is the ambiguity of the lexical item light. Since an adequate dictionary entry for a lexical item must mark every one of its senses, the dictionary entry for light must represent it as at least two-ways ambiguous, in terms of two readings which differ from each other in that one contains the semantic marker (Color) but not the semantic marker (Weight) and the other contains (Weight) but not (Color). Since there is nothing in (2) to exclude either one of these readings as genuine readings for the occurrence of light, the sentence is semantically ambiguous, one term of this ambiguity stemming from each of these readings.

However, the presence of an ambiguous lexical item in a syntactically unambiguous sentence is not a sufficient condition for that sentence to be semantically ambiguous. For example, although the sentence

(3) the stuff is light enough to carry

contains an occurrence of the ambiguous lexical item light, it is not itself ambiguous because light enough to carry is not understood to mean 'light enough in color to be carried'. Thus when there is an ambiguous lexical item in a semantically unambiguous sentence, either the syntactic properties of the sentence or the meanings of the other constituents prevent the ambiguous lexical item from contributing more than one of its senses to the meaning of the whole sentence.

Selection of some senses of a lexical item, with the consequent exclusion of others, is of fundamental importance because, together with lexical ambiguity, it determines what meaning a sentence is given by the semantic interpretation which the semantic component assigns it. Therefore, each reading in the dictionary entry for a lexical item must contain a selection restriction, i.e., a formally expressed necessary and sufficient condition for that reading to combine with others. Thus, the selection restriction attached to a reading determines the combinations with the readings of other lexical items into which that reading can enter when a projection rule is applied.

We may regard such selection restrictions as the explication for certain features of standard dictionary practice. The formal representation of selection restrictions is a device for indicating

such information as The Shorter Oxford English Dictionary's
qualification that the word honest when applied generally means
'of good moral character, virtuous, upright', while when applied
to women it means both this and 'chaste'.

Selection restrictions are formulated as functions of syntactic
or semantic markers. For example, let us take the case of a
selection restriction for semantically acceptable combinations
of the readings for a modifier and for the head which it modifies.
If the readings in the dictionary entry for the lexical item honest
are correctly formulated, then one of them will be: honest →
Adjective → (Evaluative) → (Moral) → [Innocent of illicit sexual
intercourse] ⟨(Human) and (Female)⟩. The selection restriction in this reading is construed as saying that an adjectival occurrence of the lexical item honest bears the sense (Evaluative)
→ (Moral) → [Innocent of illicit sexual intercourse] just in case
the reading for the nominal head which this adjectival occurrence
modifies contains both the semantic marker (Human) and the semantic marker (Female). If the reading for this nominal head
lacks one or both of these markers, no combination occurs, and
there is no derived reading which represents the meaning of the
modifier-head constituent in terms of the meanings of its components. Thus, an expression such as honest woman, in one of
its senses, means 'a woman who is not guilty of illicit sexual
intercourse' because the lexical item woman has a reading containing both (Human) and (Female). But an expression such as
honest geranium has no meaning because the reading of the lexical item geranium fails to satisfy the selection restriction for
honest. In cases where syntactically compound expressions are
assigned no derived reading, we shall say that the semantic component marks them as semantically anomalous.

The formulation of a dictionary for the semantic component
of a particular language can be greatly economized by taking advantage of a relation between certain pairs of semantic markers.
The relation that serves this purpose is the category inclusion
relation which holds between a pair of semantic markers when
the category represented by one is a subcategory of that represented by the other. For example, the semantic marker (Human)
represents a conceptual category that is included in the categories
represented by (Animate), (Higher Animal), (Physical Object),
etc., but the category that the semantic marker (Physical Object) represents is not included in any of these other aforementioned categories. These category inclusion relations will be
specified within the general theory of linguistic descriptions as
part of that theory's statement of the semantic concepts that
are linguistic universals when such a statement is a true generalization about the structure of the dictionary for every linguistic
description. Should such a relation between a pair of semantic

markers hold within some but not all dictionaries, then the relation
must be stated only within and for those dictionaries. Nevertheless, stating it once at the beginning of the dictionary affords a
significant simplification.[8]

The advantage in economy that results from taking category
inclusion relations between semantic markers into account in
constructing a dictionary is as follows. When a reading in a dictionary entry contains a semantic marker (M_2) which is specified
(in the general theory of linguistic descriptions or in the dictionary for a given semantic component) as representing a category
that is included in the category represented by the semantic marker (M_1), then this reading need not mention (i.e., explicitly contain) the marker (M_1), since membership in the category represented by (M_1) is implicitly determined by the presence of (M_2).
This means that for every category inclusion relation which is
not stated reading by reading but rather is stated by a category
inclusion rule which expresses the fact that the category C_i represented by (M_i) is included in the category C_j represented by (M_j),
the dictionary saves one symbol for each reading which contains
(M_j). For the entire dictionary there is thus an enormous saving
achieved by avoiding redundancy in specifying the semantic elements from which the meanings of lexical items are built. But
it should be stressed that such economy, though sufficient, is
not the sole motivation for generating parts of lexical readings
by rules. Just as significant is the fact that such rules enable
either particular linguistic descriptions or the general theory
of linguistic descriptions to state certain abstract truths about
the dictionary entries of particular languages and about universal semantic facts of all languages. The considerations concerning the minimization of symbols in the dictionary, which
lead to the use of rules for generating parts of lexical readings,
are a formal indication of the fact that such rules express true
generalizations about the semantic properties of languages. That
is, these simplicity considerations force us to add to the semantic component rules representing, for example, the fact that the
category of human objects is included in the category of animate
objects.

Category inclusion rules will be formulated so as to apply to
a reading in a dictionary entry in maximally economical form.
They will expand the reading by introducing into it for a semantic marker (M_n) every semantic marker (M_1), (M_2), ..., (M_{n-1})
that, according to the rules, represents a category including
(M_n). These rules will apply just after Condition (i), given on
page 18, applies. Thus the category inclusion rules will operate
on the readings assigned to the lowest nodes of underlying P-
markers and will expand these readings at that point. The need
to have nodes of P-markers associated with readings in expanded

form will become clear when we show how semantic properties
of constituents are to be marked in terms of the readings assigned
to the P-markers of these sentences.[9]

Having considered the character of the dictionary, we now turn
to the process of assigning a semantic interpretation to a sentence, i. e. , to the operation of the projection rules. The syntactic component provides the semantic component with the input of a sentence such as

(4) the boy likes candy

and an associated P-marker of the form shown in Diagram 2.8.

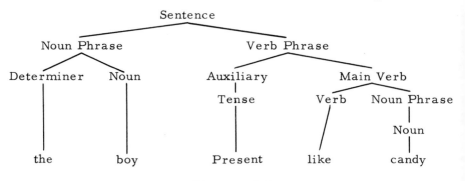

Diagram 2.8

The first step that the semantic component performs in providing a semantic interpretation for (4) is to associate with each of
the lexical items in (4) — i. e. , with the, boy, like, Present,
candy — all, and only, the readings from their dictionary entries that are compatible with the syntactic categorization of
these items in the P-marker represented by Diagram 2.8.

Such an association is affected by the following condition:

(i) If a reading from the dictionary entry for the lexical
     item m_j contains syntactic markers which attribute to
     m_j the same syntactic categorization that an occurrence
     of m_j has in the P-marker P^i, then this reading is as-
     signed to the set of readings R^i_j associated with the oc-
     currence of m_j in P^i.

Thus, the lexical item m_1 is associated with the set of readings
R^i_1, m_2 is associated with R^i_2, and so on. Referring back to
Diagram 2.8, we may picture the result of applying (i) as that
of converting Diagram 2.8 into one in which the lexical item the
is associated with a set of readings from its dictionary entry,
boy is associated with a set of readings from its dictionary entry, the morpheme Present is associated with a set of readings
from its entry, and so on. Thus, for example, the set of read-

ings associated with <u>candy</u> in Diagram 2.8 contains readings representing each of the senses that <u>candy</u> has as a Noun but none of
the senses that it has as a Verb, e.g., the sense <u>candy</u> has in

(5) the fruits candy easily

The next stage in the process after the category inclusion rules
have operated on the output of (i) is to combine the expanded readings to form derived readings, which are then combined with
other derived readings, until derived readings that express the
meanings of the whole sentence are obtained.

It has always been clear that syntactic structure <u>somehow</u> plays
a crucial role in a speaker's understanding of what the sentences
of his language mean.   This role is most evident in cases where
two sentences have the same meaning by virtue not only of their
lexical content but also of the syntactic relation between them
and in cases where synonymous sentences are constituted of the
same set of lexical items but differ in the arrangement of this
lexical material.   An example of the former case is

(6) a.   John plays tennis better than Joe plays tennis
     b.   John plays tennis better than Joe

An example of the latter case is

(7) a.   Washington and New York are cities
     b.   New York and Washington are cities

An example involving both cases is

(8) a.   John looked up the number
     b.   John looked the number up

The exact sense in which syntactic structure plays a role in the
speaker's understanding of a sentence can be fully appreciated
by considering the way the projection rules operate to combine
readings for lexical items and readings for higher-level constituents to produce readings for a whole sentence.

The syntactic structure of a sentence, by providing the formal
relations between the lexical items, determines what possible
combinations of meanings there are in the sentence.   Thus the
characterization of the syntactic structure given by SD from the
syntactic component determines, in part, how the semantic information from the dictionary entries associated with the lexical
items is combined by the projection rules.   In the case of Diagram 2.8, the syntactic structure permits the combination of
readings from the set of readings associated with <u>the</u> and the set
associated with <u>boy</u> and the combination of readings from the set
associated with the morpheme Present, the set associated with
<u>like</u>, and the set associated with <u>candy</u>. This structure also per-
mits the combination of the derived readings which result when

the former and latter combinations are made. But this structure
does not permit, for example, the combination of readings from
the set associated with <u>the</u> and <u>likes</u>.

   Another way of regarding the fact that the possible combinations
of readings are determined by syntactic structure stems from a
general condition of adequacy that must be imposed upon the semantic interpretation of a sentence. The semantic interpretations produced by the semantic component constitute the linguistic description's entire account of the semantic structure of a
language. Thus the semantic interpretation of a sentence is under the empirical requirement to characterize the meaning of
<u>each and every</u> constituent (in the P-marker(s) whose nodes are
assigned readings) of the sentence, and not to characterize the
meaning for any substring of the sentence that is not one of its
constituents. If a semantic theory failed to characterize the meaning of some constituent of a sentence, then since a speaker is able
to determine meanings not only for whole sentences but also for
their significant subparts, the theory would be to that extent incomplete. For example, the semantic interpretation of the sentence

   (9) the man hit the ball

must represent the meaning of the constituents of this sentence,
i.e., <u>the</u>, <u>man</u>, <u>hit</u>, <u>the</u>, <u>ball</u>, <u>the man</u>, <u>hit the ball</u>, and <u>the man</u>
<u>hit the ball</u>. But it must not provide any meaning for such sub-
strings of (9) as <u>the man hit</u> or <u>hit the</u>. Obviously, this condition
of adequacy can be fulfilled only if the syntactic component provides, for each sentence it generates, and enumeration of all, and
only, its constituents.

   In terms of a transformational syntactical component, the 'syntactic structure' of a sentence is given by the set of P-markers
and the T-marker in its SD. The constituents of a sentence are
given in its P-markers as just those substrings which are dominated by a node in one of these P-markers. Therefore, the combinations of meanings which the projection rules accomplish are
determined by the bracketing relations in the P-markers of sentences. Whenever two meanings are combined to form a derived
meaning, this meaning is assigned as the reading for the node
immediately dominating the two constituents whose meanings were
combined.

   <u>Type 1 projection rules</u> (henceforth P1) produce derived readings by combining the readings of lower-order constituents to
form readings for higher-order constituents. They affect a series
of amalgamations of readings, proceeding from the bottom to the
top of a P-marker by embedding readings into one another to form
a new reading, the <u>derived reading</u>. The derived reading is assigned to the set of readings associated with the node that im-

mediately dominates the sets of readings from which those amalgamated were drawn. The derived reading provides one of the
meanings for the sequence of lexical items dominated by the node
to which this derived reading is assigned. In this manner, a set
of alternative meanings is provided for every constituent of a
sentence, until the highest constituent, Sentence, is reached and
associated with a set of derived readings that provide the meanings for the whole sentence.

Amalgamation is the operation of forming a composite reading
made up of a reading from each of the sets of readings dominated
by a given node in a P-marker. A pair of readings is joined if
one of them satisfies the selection restriction in the other. Sup-
pose that a node labeled by a syntactic marker SM dominates just
the sets of readings R_1^i, R_2^i, ..., R_n^i, where the first of these
sets contains k_1 readings, the second contains k_2 readings, ...,
and the nth contains k_m readings. Then the set of derived readings that is associated with the node labeled by SM contains at
most $(k_1 \times k_2 \times ... \times k_m)$ members, and possibly zero members
if selection restrictions prevent every syntactically possible combination from forming.

Each member of the set of readings assigned to a dominating
node is a reading for the lexical string that this marker dominates in the P-marker. The number of readings that is thus allotted to a constituent is the degree of its semantic ambiguity:
a constituent that is allotted no readings is anomalous, one with
exactly one reading is unambiguous, and one with two or more
readings is semantically ambiguous in two or more ways.

An example of a Pl is the following:

(R1)   Given two readings associated with nodes branching
       from the same node labeled SM, one of the form,

Lexical string$_1$ → syntactic markers of head → (a_1) →
(a_2) → ... → (a_n) → $[1]$ $\langle 1 \rangle$

and the other of the form,

Lexical string$_2$ → syntactic markers of modifier of
head → (b_1) → (b_2) → ... → (b_m) → $[2]$ $\langle 2 \rangle$

such that the string of syntactic or semantic markers
of the head has a substring which satisfies $\langle 2 \rangle$,
then there is a derived reading of the form,

Lexical string$_2$ + Lexical string$_1$ → SM → (a_1) → (a_2)
→ ... → (a_n) → (b_1) → (b_2) → ... → (b_m) → $[[2][1]]$
$\langle 1 \rangle$;

where any occurrence of the same semantic marker
or distinguisher, except the first, is erased. This
derived reading is assigned to the set of readings associated with SM.[10]

An example of an amalgamation produced by (R1) is the join-
ing of the reading colorful → Adjective → (Color) → [Abounding
in contrast or variety of bright colors] ⟨ (Physical Object) v
(Social Activity)⟩ and the reading ball → Noun → (Physical Object) → (Globular Shape) to produce the derived reading colorful
+ ball → (Physical Object) → (Globular Shape) → (Color) → [Abound-
ing in contrast or variety of bright colors]. This derived reading gives the sense that colorful ball has in the sentence

(10) the baby is playing with a colorful ball

An example of an amalgamation that is prevented by a selection
restriction is that of the reading colorful → Adjective → (Evaluative) → [Having distinctive character, vividness, or picturesque-
ness] ⟨ (Aesthetic Object) v (Social Activity) ⟩ with the reading
for ball given immediately above. This is precluded because the
selection restriction in the reading of the modifier allows it to
be embedded in readings for heads only if the reading for a head
contains either the semantic marker (Aesthetic Object) or the
semantic marker (Social Activity) or both, and this reading of
ball contains neither of these semantic markers.

Thus (R1) explicates the process of attribution, i.e., the process of creating a new semantic unit, from a modifier and a head,
whose semantic properties are those of the head, except that the
compound has a more determinate meaning than does the head
by virtue of the semantic information contributed by the modifier.
The information about modifier-head relations which must be
available to (R1) in order for it to operate properly will be supplied by the syntactic component (in a manner which will be discussed later).

We introduce here the notion semantically interpreted P-marker, which we define as a set of pairs with respect to the P-marker, one member of which is a node of the P-marker and the other
of which is a set of readings, each reading giving one of the meanings of the string dominated by that node in the P-marker. The
set of readings for each node is maximal in the sense that every
reading for the string which can belong to this set on the basis
of the dictionary, projection rules, and syntactic structure is,
in fact, a member of this set, and only these are members. The
P1 operate to produce semantically interpreted P-markers.

In early statements of transformational grammar much emphasis was placed on the distinction between sentences that had
only obligatory singulary transformations in their T-marker and
sentences which had also[11] at least one optional singulary transformation or at least one generalized transformation. The former
were called kernel sentences.[12]

Originally P1 were designed to operate on the final derived
P-markers of kernel sentences. Whether or not they would also

operate on other P-markers was not determined. In particular,
it was not decided whether P1 would operate on the P-markers
produced by the operation of optional singulary transformations.
As these transformations were formulated in the literature, it
was noted that many of them never changed meaning, i.e., the
transform had the same meaning as the structure that was transformed to obtain it. In order to account for regularities of this
kind, it was suggested that such transformations be regarded as
establishing equivalence classes of sentences, such that, for any
set of transformations T_1, T_2, ..., T_n and any sequence of sentences s_1, s_2, ..., s_n, where s_1 is a kernel and s_2 comes from
s_1 by T_1, s_3 from s_2 by T_2, ..., s_n from s_{n-1} by T_n, s_1, s_2, ...,
s_n, all belong to the same equivalence class. Then, since at
least one member of such equivalence classes (the kernel) already had a semantically interpreted P-marker which provided
a meaning for the sentence and since all sentences in the equivalence class have the same meaning, one could express these regularities by introducing the convention that every member of such
an equivalence class has the same semantically interpreted P-
marker. This device made the use of P1 unnecessary in all such
cases of optional singulary transformations.[13]
    On the other hand, in the case of optional singulary transforma-
tions that do change meaning (assuming there are such) and in the
case of generalized transformations, an alternative to using P1
to produce semantically interpreted P-markers was allowed for.
Type 2 projection rules (henceforth P2) were originally intended
to explicate the manner in which such transformations alter or
build up meanings. Moreover, P2 were intended as a way of
stating in the semantic component what effect transformations
have on the meanings of the structures they operate on, and how
systematic these effects are from one type of transformation to
another. These P2 were characterized as rules which derive a
semantically interpreted P-marker for a sentence S that results
from an optional singulary transformation that affects meaning,
or from a generalized transformation, on the basis of the interpreted P-markers of the kernels that underlie S. Meanings for
a constituent are derived by P1 so as to reflect the manner in
which those meanings were composed from the meanings of subconstituents and their phrase structure. The P2 were to derive
meanings for a sentence so as to reflect the manner in which those
meanings were composed from the meanings of the sentence struc-
ture(s) used in its transformational derivation as well as the character of this derivation.
    Now consider the concept semantic interpretation of a sentence.
It is common to speak of the syntax as generating 'sentences'.
This usage is, however, ambiguous. Because of the phenomenon
of syntactic ambiguity the same string of formatives is often pro-

vided with two or more distinct SD by the syntax. For example, the string

(11) I like little boys and girls

receives at least two different SD one of which contains the P-marker in Diagram 2.9, the other of which contains the P-marker in Diagram 2.10. The semantic interpretation of 'sentences' is

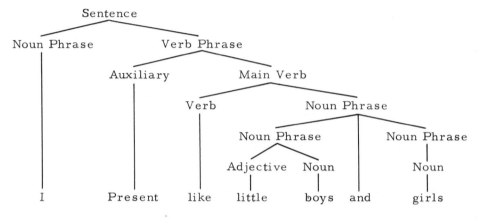

Diagram 2.9

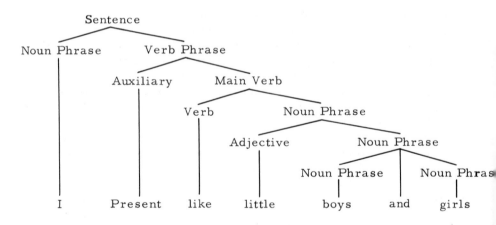

Diagram 2.10

concerned with 'sentence' not in the ambiguous sense in which this term may denote two or more distinct SD but rather in the sense in which 'sentence' refers to a string of formatives with a fixed SD. Henceforth, to avoid this ambiguity we use the term 'sentence' to refer to a fixed string of formatives regardless of the SD it receives. We introduce the term sentoid to refer to a string of formatives with a unique associated SD. Sentoids are thus unambiguous syntactically and represent the truly independent objects generated by the syntactic component. Thus (11) represents one sentence but two sentoids.

In terms of this distinction, we define the <u>semantic interpretation of a sentence</u> S to be: (1) the set of semantically interpreted P-markers such that each semantically interpreted P-marker represents one of the n ways in which S is syntactically ambiguous, i.e., one of the n different sentoids that S represents; and (2) the set of statements about S that follow from this definition schema:

> S is <u>fully</u> X if and only if S is X on every semantically interpreted P-marker in each sentoid which S represents.

In order to complete this definition of the notion <u>semantic interpretation of a sentence</u>, it is necessary to determine the semantic properties over which the variable X in the above schema ranges. That is to say, it is necessary to determine what semantic properties of sentoids the semantic interpretations produced by the semantic component should mark.

The semantic description of a sentoid must represent the meaning of every constituent of the sentoid in such a manner that, in the first place, it marks semantically ambiguous sentoids, and marks semantically ambiguous constituents of sentences. For example, the sentoid represented by

(12) the bank is the scene of the crime

is semantically ambiguous between meanings, among which are the one in which <u>bank</u> has the sense of 'an establishment for monetary exchange', the one in which <u>bank</u> has the sense of 'a steep acclivity or slope', the one in which <u>bank</u> has the sense of 'the rising ground bordering a body of water', etc. An adequate semantic component must mark (12) as at least three-ways semantically ambiguous, and must mark its Noun Phrase subject as also three-ways semantically ambiguous.

Second, the semantic interpretation of a sentoid must mark it as semantically anomalous or semantically acceptable depending on whether the meanings of its constituents can combine so as to yield a cognitively coherent meaning for the whole sentoid. For example,

(13) the paint is silent

is anomalous, whereas

(14) he paints silently

is semantically acceptable, and a semantic interpretation of these sentoids must so characterize them.

Third, the semantic interpretation of a sentoid must mark semantic relations between that sentoid and others, even though they may differ widely in syntactic structure or morphemic constitution.

For example, semantic interpretations of

(15) eye-doctors eye blonds

(16) oculists eye blonds

(17) blonds are eyed by eye-doctors

must mark them as paraphrases of each other, but must mark

(18) eye-doctors eye what gentlemen prefer

as not a paraphrase of either (15), (16), or (17).

Fourth, semantic interpretations must mark sentoids represented by such strings as

(19) blonds like redheads

(20) blonds do not like redheads

as inconsistent with each other. In other words, one of these
sentoids is true if and only if the other is false.

Finally, the semantic interpretation of a sentoid must indicate
such semantic properties as whether or not the sentoid is analytic, synthetic, or contradictory. A sentoid is analytic if it is true
by virtue of meaning alone.[14] A sentoid is contradictory if it is
false by virtue of meaning alone. A synthetic sentoid cannot be
established as true or false solely on grounds of meaning but requires some comparison of what the sentoid asserts with what is
empirically the case. Thus the semantic interpretations of

(21) spinsters are women

(22) spinsters are nice

(23) spinsters are married

must mark them, respectively, as analytic, synthetic, and contradictory.

Semantic properties of sentoids, such as those just discussed,
can be marked in terms of formal features of semantically interpreted P-markers with the following definitions. Let S be some
sentoid, specified in terms of its semantically interpreted P-
marker PM, and let C and C′ be any two distinct constituents of
S. Then

(D1) C is semantically anomalous with respect to PM if
and only if the set of readings associated with the node
labeled 'C' in PM contains no readings, i.e., is null.

(D2) C is semantically unambiguous with respect to PM if
and only if the set of readings associated with the node
labeled 'C' in PM contains exactly one member.

(D3) C is n-ways semantically ambiguous with respect to

PM if and only if the set of readings associated with
the node labeled 'C' in PM contains n members, for
n greater than or equal to 2.

(D4)   C and C′ are <u>synonymous on a reading</u> with respect to
PM and PM′ if and only if the set of readings associated
with the node labeled 'C' in PM and the set of readings
associated with the node labeled 'C′' in PM′ have at
least one member in common; PM may equal PM′.

(D5)   C and C′ are <u>fully synonymous</u> with respect to PM and
PM′ if and only if the set of readings associated with
the node labeled 'C' in PM and the set of readings associated with the node labeled 'C′' in PM′ are identical;
PM may equal PM′.

It should be pointed out that (D4) and (D5) are, respectively,
definitions for the concepts <u>paraphrase on a reading</u> with respect
to PM and PM′ and <u>full paraphrase</u> with respect to PM and PM′
also, since they define these latter concepts if C is the constituent
Sentence. It should also be made clear that definitions (D1) through
(D5) are not sufficient to cover all the semantic properties that
have to be marked in the semantic interpretations of an empirically adequate semantic component. We have explicitly left out
definitions for such semantic properties as <u>analyticity</u>, <u>contra-</u>
<u>diction</u>, and <u>entailment</u> because these definitions are not self-
explanatory in the way that (D1) through (D5) clearly are.[15]

From (D1) through (D5), one can obtain a fairly clear idea of
how the range of the variable X in the definition schema is determined. We have then characterized the notion of a semantic interpretation of a sentence as completely as is necessary for our
study.

NOTES

1. Chomsky (1955a, 1957, 1961, 1962, 1964 b).

2. We extend the notion <u>dominate</u> in such a way that A will be
    said to dominate B where B is part of some string which is
    an A. For a more precise and detailed discussion of phrase
    structure rules, P-markers, P-marker assignment, etc.,
    cf. Chomsky (1955a, 1959, 1963 b) and Postal (1964).

3. These and all other exemplificatory P-markers in this study
    are greatly oversimplified whenever this does not affect the
    point under discussion, and they should not be taken as mak-
    ing claims beyond those made in the text.

4. It appears that in underlying P-markers there are no struc-
    tural ambiguities, i.e., cases where the same string of mor-

phemes is dominated by two different constituents. Such ambiguity is, however, a pervading feature of final derived P-markers and actual sentences and is thus due to transformational operations.

5. For a more adequate and detailed account of transformational rules, cf. Chomsky (1955 a, 1957, 1961, 1962, 1964 b).

6. Katz and Fodor (1963).

7. The fact that meanings are analyzable into subcomponents is the chief insight and basis for so-called 'componential analysis', an approach to semantics that has developed in anthropology. Cf. Lounsbury (1956), Goodenough (1951, 1956), Wallace and Atkins (1960), etc. However, such studies have failed to recognize that the analyzability of meanings extends beyond certain limited lexical sets like kinship terms, body parts, etc., to include all lexical items. More importantly, work in componential analysis of individual lexical items or sets has not shown how the componential analysis of such items may be integrated in a full linguistic description which supplies semantic interpretations for each of the infinite set of well-formed sentences and their constituents. This gap is due largely to the failure to consider the need for projection rules and the failure to consider componential analysis within the context of explicit generative linguistic descriptions.

8. Of course, this relation of category inclusion is not the only relation that will be specified universally within the general theory of linguistic descriptions or within the dictionary as a condition governing the whole dictionary. For another example of such a relation between semantic markers, cf. Katz (in preparation b), where the relation of antonymy that holds, for example, between (Male) and (Female) is discussed.

9. There is a direct analogy between these category inclusion rules of semantics and the morpheme structure rules in phonology that do not operate on linear contexts. Cf. Halle (1959, 1962), Chomsky and Miller (1963).

10. The erasure clause in (R1) is included to avoid pointlessly duplicating semantic markers and distinguishers in the derived reading. Thus, for example, it makes no sense to include the semantic markers (Human) and (Female) twice in the reading associated with the compound expression spinster aunt just because each of the readings combined contains occurrences of both these markers. In the derived reading for spinster aunt one occurrence of each of these markers is sufficient; another occurrence of each adds no semantic information.

11. There were not, as has sometimes been erroneously as-
     sumed (cf. Dixon [1963], p. 69), any sentences derived
     without any transformations at all.

12. Cf. Chomsky (1957), p. 45.

13. For these positions, cf. Katz and Fodor (1963).

14. Quine (1953).

15. Katz (1964 b).

Chapter 3

PROJECTION RULES

3.1 Introduction

The account of the semantic component in Chapter 2 leaves at
least two fundamental questions about the projection rules unanswered.

First, there is the question of <u>which</u> P-markers in the set of
all P-markers assigned to a string of formatives in a sentoid by
its SD the Pl operate on in giving that sentoid a semantic interpretation. For example, the Pl might operate on only the underlying P-marker(s), or on only the final derived P-marker, or on
all of the P-markers, or on some proper subset of the set of all
P-markers. The choice made here determines whether or not
P2 are in fact required in the semantic component and also, if
they are required, at what point they restrict the range of application of Pl. If Pl operate on <u>all</u> the P-markers in a sentoid,
then it is clear that no P2 will be needed in the semantic component. If the Pl operate on some but not all the P-markers of a
sentoid, then, depending upon which P-markers they operate on,
P2 may be needed to provide a semantic interpretation for those
P-markers which are not operated on by Pl.

Second, there is the question of the form of P2 should such
rules prove necessary. The Pl have this general form: Given
two readings associated, respectively, with two nodes branching from the same node in a P-marker, one reading being of the
form Rl and the other of the form R2, such that Rl has a substring which satisfies the selection restriction in R2, there is
a derived reading with R2 embedded in Rl in such and such a
manner. This second question, then, concerns the analogous
characterization of the form of P2.

In the present chapter we propose definite answers to both of
these questions and discuss some of the implications of these
answers.

Corresponding to the syntactic distinction between singulary
and generalized transformations is a fundamental semantic distinction between two different types of question about the semantic correlates of transformations. With respect to singulary
transformations, it makes sense to ask whether or not they alter or affect meaning and, if so, how. But for generalized transformations this question makes no sense. Here one can only ask

how the meanings of the input structures are combined to yield a
meaning for the output. Because of this distinction, then, it is
necessary to break the question about the range of P1 into two
parts: one concerned with the semantic interpretation of the structures derived by singulary transformations alone, the other with
the semantic interpretation of those whose derivation involves
generalized transformations.

3.2 Semantic Interpretation of Structures Derived Solely by Singulary Transformations

Among those sentences derived solely with singulary transformations are the set whose T-markers contain only obligatory
transformations, i.e., the kernel sentences of earlier transformational discussions. It is universally agreed that such transformations have no semantic effects, and it is clear why this
must be so. The output of sentences which result from such
rules is fully determined by the input P-markers. Hence, the
question of utilizing P2 in the semantic interpretation of such
sentences does not arise. Even if the semantic component does
contain P2, the P2 do not operate here. Sentences with only obligatory singulary transformations in their T-markers must be
semantically interpreted by P1 alone. The question still remaining concerns which P-markers the P1 operate on in such cases.
In previous discussions, it was assumed that in these cases P1
operate on the final derived P-markers. This assumption provided a straightforward formalization of the principle that P2
play no role in the semantic interpretation of such sentences.
We shall see, however, that there are grounds for changing this
stipulation of the range of P1 in kernel sentences and that the new
statement of the range of P1 provides an equally formal representation of the fact that kernel sentences are interpreted fully
without P2.

There are many treatments of grammatical facts in the literature that involve optional singulary transformations not affecting
the meaning of the structures on which they operate. This is true
of transformations describing cases of alternative word order
like

(1) the student looked up the word

(2) the student looked the word up

those describing the passive construction, those describing negation (in Klima's or Lees's treatment),[1] etc. In all these cases
it is clear that the semantic interpretations of the P-markers
which result from transformational applications must, if correct,
be the same as those which were transformed.

But there are also many cases in the literature of syntactic
facts characterized by optional singulary transformations where
the output P-marker must have a semantic interpretation quite
different from that of the input P-marker. Among these are the
question transformation, the imperative transformation, the wh̄
attachment transformation, etc.[2] Thus there are three possibilities: first, that no <u>correctly formulated</u> singulary transformation has an output with a semantic interpretation distinct from
its input and that those transformations in the literature which
violate this claim are incorrect; second, that all singulary transformations affect meaning and those in the literature which do
not are incorrect; third, that some do and some do not affect semantic interpretation and it is some specific feature of the particular transformations that determines which do and which do
not.

The first two alternatives are clearly preferable, even though
what at present appear to be the facts throw more doubt upon
them than upon the third, because they make no reference to
specific features of a class of transformations. Thus the first
two provide a more general account of how sentences containing
only singulary transformations in their T-markers are semantically interpreted. Of <u>these</u> two alternatives, the first is preferable to the second for exactly the same reason that both are preferable to the third. If the generalization that <u>no</u> singulary transformation affects meaning can be established, it will provide the
most general account of how sentences with only singulary transformations in their T-markers are interpreted, because, unlike
the contrary alternative, it will not be necessary to make a special proviso for the case of <u>obligatory</u> singulary transformations.

Thus, on a priori methodological grounds, the first of the three
alternatives is the one which deserves to be provisionally accepted.
This alternative claims that P2 play no role in the semantic interpretation of any sentoid without a generalized transformation
in its T-marker. This still leaves unanswered, of course, the
question of which P-markers in such sentoids the P1 operate on.

The conclusions reached thus far leave us with two important
tasks. First, it is necessary to construct the formal conceptual
apparatus for the semantic component which will represent in
the most economical and natural manner the generalization that
no singulary transformation affects meaning, i.e., that sentences
without generalized transformations in their T-markers are fully
interpreted semantically by P1 alone. This apparatus must provide a decision as to which of the P-markers in the SD of a sentence derived without generalized transformations are semantically interpreted by P1. Second, we must defend the generalization that singulary transformations are semantically irrelevant
by showing that those transformational analyses whose present

formulation is incompatible with it are incorrect. Also it is necessary to defend our particular choice of conceptual apparatus
against other possibilities.

Among the possible kinds of conceptual apparatus for expressing the generalization that singulary transformations do not affect
meaning, there are several devices. It is possible to have sentoids without generalized transformations in their T-markers
fully interpreted by having Pl operate: (a) only on their final derived P-markers; (b) on all of their P-markers; and (c) only on
their underlying P-markers. We choose (c) because it most naturally expresses the generalization that no singulary transformation has a semantic effect. It effectively says that none of the
syntactic changes produced by the operation of singulary transformations on underlying P-markers are relevant to the meaning
of the resulting structures. Furthermore, (c) seems to be the
most natural and intuitive choice because, as noted earlier, derived P-markers are completely determined by underlying P-
markers and T-markers, and hence derived P-markers contain
no independent information.

We now turn to substantive arguments supporting the claim
that Pl must operate only on underlying P-markers in the case
of sentences derived without generalized transformations.

A crucial syntactic fact about languages is that there are sets
of sentences whose underlying P-markers are similar or identical although their derived P-markers may be radically different
and conversely that there are other sets of sentences whose derived P-markers are similar or identical although their underlying P-markers may be quite different. Of overwhelming importance here is the fact that similarities and differences among the
fundamental grammatical relations like 'subject', 'object', 'pred-
icate', etc., correlate only with the features of underlying P-
markers. For an example of the first type, consider these sentences:

(3) John drank the milk

(4) the milk was drunk by John

(5) who hit someone

(6) who did someone hit

It is evident to any speaker of English that in both (3) and (4) the
relation of both John and the milk to the verb drank/drunk is the
same, i.e., in each case John is the 'subject' of this verb while
the milk is the 'object'. Yet there is no feature of the otherwise
formally motivated derived P-markers for (3) and (4) that can
represent this relation. Similarly, in (5) it is evident that who
is the 'subject' of hit while in (6) the pronoun is the 'object' of
that verb. Further, in these cases it is evident that in (5) someone is the 'object' of hit while in (6) it is the 'subject'. Yet again

there are no features of the derived P-markers of (5) and (6) which can represent in a non-ad hoc way[3] the relational equivalence between who in (5) and someone in (6) and who in (6) and someone in (5).

However, although the derived P-markers of (3) through (6) do not represent the similarities in grammatical relations found in them, the underlying P-markers for these sentences provided by a transformational syntactic component can. Examples (3) through (6) will have, respectively, the underlying P-markers[4] shown in Diagrams 3.1-3.4. But now in such P-markers it is possible to give a natural characterization of general grammatical relations like 'subject', etc. In accordance with Chomsky,[5] they can be characterized in terms of subconfigurations of constituents in P-markers. Thus for English at least the 'subject' relation can be defined in terms of the configuration (Sentence: Noun

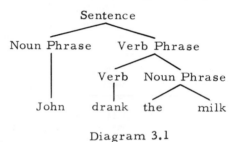

Diagram 3.1

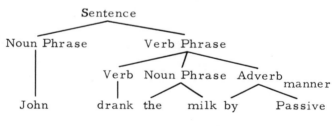

Diagram 3.2

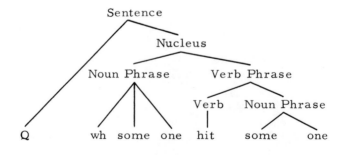

Diagram 3.3

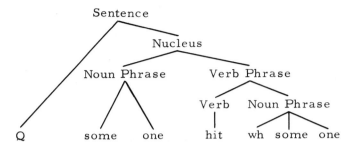

Diagram 3.4

Phrase + Verb Phrase), in which case it holds between any string
of morphemes dominated by such a Noun Phrase and the string
dominated by the following Verb Phrase if the sequence of such
strings is dominated by Sentence. Thus the 'subject' relation
will hold between John and drank the milk in the underlying P-
markers of (3) and (4) and hence for the appropriate items in the
actual sentences of (3) and (4) since the grammatical relations
of a sentoid are those of its underlying P-marker(s). On the
other hand, the 'object' relation might be defined as the configuration [Verb Phrase: Verb + Noun Phrase + (Adverb ...)], in
which case it will hold between drank/drunk and the milk in (3)
and (4) and between the appropriate elements of (5) and (6). Thus
the configurational approach to grammatical relations based on
underlying P-markers can account for intuitive similarities in
relations among strings of superficially different structure without the recognition of ad hoc elements or notions.

Similarly, this approach accounts in the most natural and general way for differences in grammatical relations among strings
with superficially similar structures. Consider the contrast between these sentences:

(7) the picture was painted by a new student

(8) the picture was painted by a new technique

It is evident that in (7) a new student is the subject of paint, while
in (8) the actual subject is not expressed and a new technique is
a modifier of the verb. Hence, (7) is a full paraphrase of

(9) a new student painted the picture

while (8) and the ungrammatical

(10)* a new technique painted the picture

---

* Examples preceded by asterisk are not well formed, i. e.,
are ungrammatical.

are not paraphrases at all. These facts about grammatical relations, however, obviously cannot be expressed in any non-ad hoc
way by the derived P-markers of (7) and (8). But the underlying
P-markers of (7) and (8) are as shown in Diagrams 3.5 and 3.6,
respectively.[6] In these structures the correct grammatical re-

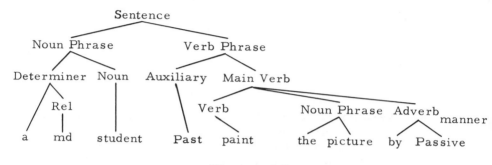

Diagram 3.5

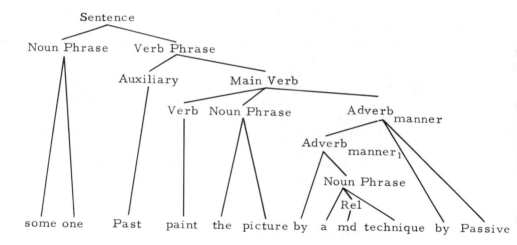

Diagram 3.6

lations are automatically given by the configurational technique.
Example (8) has a pronominal subject which is later deleted after
the passive transformation has applied. Example (7) has as subject a Noun Phrase with a head student modified by a Rel which
later becomes transformationally an Adjective new. Thus in the
underlying P-markers the distinct character of the two different
by-phrases found in the actual sentences (7) and (8) is clearly
represented. In the derived P-markers, however, both phrases
would have the structure shown in Diagram 3.7, which could never
serve for semantic purposes. In one case, the Noun Phrase on
the right actually was generated there in the phrase structure.

<table>
<tr><td>Adverb</td></tr>
</table>

Adverb
    manner
by   Noun Phrase

Diagram 3.7

In the other, it is the subject Noun Phrase which replaced the passive morpheme when the passive transformation was applied.

An even more convincing case where differences in grammatical relations among strings with superficially similar structures can be explained by underlying P-markers is apparent from cases whose description actually involves generalized transformations and which thus really belong in Section 3.3. Consider the contrast between these two sentences:

(11) John is eager to please

(12) John is easy to please

or the triple ambiguity of the utterances represented by

(13) a. the killing of the tiger's
      b. the killing of the tigers'
      c. the killing of the tigers

It is evident that in (11) <u>John</u> is the subject of <u>please</u> while in (12) it is the object of this verb. In (13) the ambiguity is due to the fact that in a and b the Noun Phrase after <u>of</u> is the subject of <u>killing</u> while in c this Noun Phrase is the object of this verbal. The ambiguity between a and b is trivially explained by the presence or absence of the Plural morpheme and concomitant representation of the Genitive as either <u>null</u> or z. The only formally motivated final derived P-markers for (11) and (12) cannot account for their contrast, and the presence or absence of Genitive and Plural, which is all that differentiates the three final derived P-markers associated with (13), is clearly inadequate to explain how they are understood. (See Diagrams 3.8-3.10.) There is no information in these P-markers which can correctly characterize in a non-<u>ad hoc</u> way the differences in grammatical relations of which the speaker is aware. But in a transformational syntax it is easy to show that there are strong formal motivations

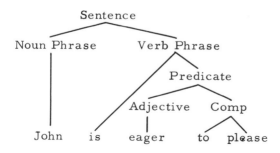

Sentence
Noun Phrase   Verb Phrase
                    Predicate
             Adjective   Comp
John   is   eager   to please

Diagram 3.8

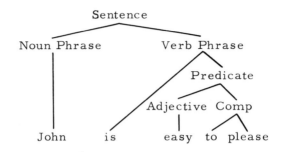

Diagram 3.9

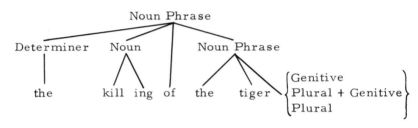

Diagram 3.10

for deriving the kinds of superficially similar derived P-markers of Diagrams 3.8 and 3.9 from distinct underlying P-markers of the forms shown in Diagrams 3.11 and 3.12, respectively, and for deriving the barely distinct P-markers of Diagram 3.10 from the pairs of distinct underlying P-markers shown in Diagrams 3.13 and 3.14, respectively. (Cf. our discussion of these derivations in Section 4.3.) But now in these the correct grammatical relations for Examples (7)-(9) are automatically given by the configurational technique already discussed. Notice that the P-markers of Diagrams 3.11-3.14 must be generated by an English grammar regardless of how (7)-(9) are described. For this reason it is clear that a transformational syntactic component can account correctly for differences in grammatical relations among strings which are superficially similar.

Thus we can conclude this discussion of the syntactic aspect of grammatical relations as follows. It appears that in the for-

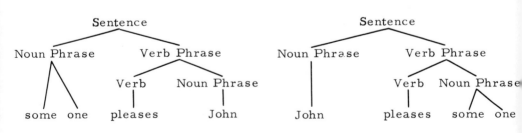

Diagram 3.11   Diagram 3.12

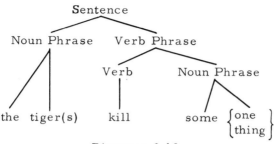

Diagram 3.13

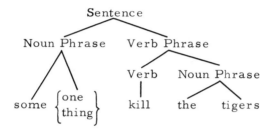

Diagram 3.14

mally motivated underlying P-markers provided by the simplest
transformational grammar there is associated with each grammatical relation a unique subconfiguration of constituents that
can be taken as the formal basis for these relations. But in derived P-markers no such unique correlation between grammatical relations and configurations of constituents can be found. This
is the most important sense in which derived P-markers provide
only a superficial account of grammatical structure, with the
'deeper' facts represented only in underlying P-markers.

The meaning of a sentence is a function not only of the meanings of its lexical items but also of the grammatical relations
between them. In the simplest case this is illustrated by

(14) John loves Mary

(15) Mary loves John

where the difference in meaning cannot be attributed to a difference in the meanings of the lexical items because they are
the same in both cases. But since the meaning of a sentence is
in part determined by the grammatical relations in it, and since,
furthermore, these relations are uniquely characterized syntactically only in underlying P-markers, it follows that P1 must obtain the meanings of a sentence from the meanings of its lexical
items by operating on underlying P-markers. Otherwise, P1 will
not have the grammatical relations needed to determine the combinations of lexical information that give the correct meaning for
the sentence as a whole.

The remaining arguments that P1 should operate exclusively on underlying P-markers are of three types, corresponding to the three different ways in which transformations distort the structure of underlying P-markers in deriving new P-markers.[7] The three different types of constituent structure distortions are those which result from permutations (and order-changing transformations generally), from deletions, and from adjunctions or additions of constant elements.

First, consider the case of order-changing transformations. This is the kind of distortion most closely related to loss of the possibility of naturally deriving grammatical relations from P-markers since the natural characterization of these relations is in terms of unique configurations of constituents not found in actual sentences. However, distortion of these relations is not the only effect of order-changing transformations which inhibits the proper operation of P1. There are a great many cases in which the final lines of derived P-markers due to order-changing transformations contain <u>interrupted lexical items</u>, i.e., those items which are assigned readings in the semantic dictionary. Take, for example, <u>look ... up</u> in

(16) he looked the number up

Clearly, quite independently of any considerations of grammatical relations, P1 cannot operate in a non-<u>ad hoc</u> and maximally simple way on the P-marker associated with (16) itself. If the semantic component is to provide a direct interpretation of the P-markers associated with cases of discontinuities like (16), there are two possible alternatives. One is that the dictionary entries for potentially discontinuous elements could be made much more complicated by the addition of extra <u>ad hoc</u> readings which are themselves enormously complex.[8] The other is the even worse alternative of trying to devise a whole new type of projection rule for these cases of discontinuous items alone. With more complex cases of lexical discontinuity, only the latter alternative is conceivable. The complexities which can be found here include the embedding of discontinuous items in between discontinuous items in between other discontinuous items with no finite bound as in

(17) he looked the number up which the boy who found the truth out knew[9]

(18) I can't imagine a more difficult book than this for you to read

Since there is no proposal about the form for such a new type of projection rule, and since none suggests itself, this possibility cannot really be seriously discussed.

Next, whatever the semantic interpretation assigned to (16),
it must be identical with that assigned to

(19) he looked up the number

because these sentences are full paraphrases of each other. The
verb in (19) is not discontinuous, and there is a single, motivated
set of readings in the dictionary for the lexical item look up.
Clearly, the best semantic theory is one which employs P1 to
assign a semantic interpretation to sentences such as (19) and
then gives the same semantic interpretation to sentences such
as (16), in some way avoiding the use of P2 or any ad hoc types
of rules (should these be devised) on the derived P-markers containing the discontinuous lexical items. But this result follows
automatically in an over-all linguistic description whose syntactic component is a transformational grammar and whose semantic component contains P1, restricted in application to underlying
P-markers. For in such a description sentences like (16) and
(19) have the same underlying P-marker with no discontinuous
elements, and the discontinuous P-marker is generated by a transformation which operates on the underlying P-marker. Thus (16)
is derived from the same P-marker which underlies (19) by the
particle inversion transformation, which inverts the particle of
a certain set of complex verbs with their Noun Phrase objects.[10]
Assignment of a fixed semantic interpretation by P1 to the underlying P-marker of (19) with the continuous lexical item look up
thus automatically provides all the desired semantic outputs for
these sentences without ad hoc machinery of either the dictionary
or the projection rule type. The restriction of P1 to underlying
P-markers in such cases thus provides both the most natural representation and an explanation of the fact that after the necessary
changes have been made, sentences with discontinuous lexical
items have the same interpretations as other sentences where
these items are not discontinuous.[11]

Another kind of discontinuity — that which involves, not discontinuous lexical items as in the previous case, but discontinuity
among strings of higher constituent types — provides further evidence for our claim that P1 must operate exclusively on the underlying P-marker(s) of sentences derived with singulary transformations. It will be recalled from Section 2.2 that a condition
of empirical adequacy on the semantic component requires that
the semantic interpretation of a sentence must provide a set of
readings for each and every one of its constituents. If, instead
of restricting P1 to underlying P-markers, we permit them to
operate on the P-markers that result from permutation transformations, the semantic component will fail to satisfy this condition. Permutation transformations radically decrease the
amount of constituent structure associated with the strings of

terminal symbols they generate. For example, in the derived
P-marker associated with

(20) the contestants have almost all been chosen

there is necessarily no representation of the fact that have ...
been chosen is the whole Auxiliary + Verb, that the contestants
... almost all is a Noun Phrase and the object, etc. Hence,
the derived P-marker associated with (20) has far too little constituent structure to provide Pl with the information necessary
to assign correct readings to each constituent. The fact that Pl
require the kind of constituent structure information which is lost
after permutation transformations transpose higher-level constituents is rather conclusive evidence that Pl must be restricted
to underlying P-markers, since these of course contain just the
required constituent structure for having Pl assign interpretations
to each constituent. Thus the underlying P-marker for (20) is
something like that shown in Diagram 3.15. But in this structure

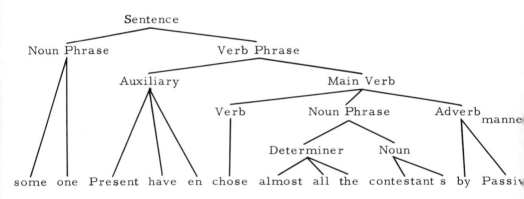

Diagram 3.15

the fact that almost all is part of a Determiner and a Noun Phrase
which is the object, and that have been chosen is the Auxiliary +
Verb, etc., is represented.

    Further evidence that cases like (20) support the view that Pl
must be restricted to underlying P-markers follows from the
observation that (20) and

(21) almost all the contestants have been chosen

are full paraphrases of each other. But as in the case of (16)
and (19), where discontinuous lexical items, rather than the discontinuous major constituents of (20) and (21), were involved,
this result is automatically obtained if Pl are restricted to underlying P-markers since (20) and (21) will certainly have the same
underlying P-marker in any correct transformational description,
namely that in Diagram 3.15.

Next let us examine deletion transformations. Consider these examples:

(22) eat the soup

(23) John plays chess as well as Sidney

These result from the application of deletion transformations to P-markers identical to those underlying[12]

(24) you will eat the soup

(25) John plays chess as well as Sidney plays chess

respectively. Examples (22) and (23) are understood as para-phrases of (24) and (25), respectively, under one interpretation of (24) — not, for example, as paraphrases respectively of

(26) he (she) will eat the soup

(27) John plays chess as well as Sidney solves problems (makes shoes)

Given these facts, there is then still another reason why P1 must not in general operate on derived P-markers. For if P1 were to operate on the derived P-markers for (22) and (23), as shown in Diagrams 3.16 and 3.17, they would not have the syntactic infor-

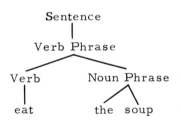

Diagram 3.16

mation they require to obtain correct semantic interpretations. The dis-tortion of the syntactic structure in the underlying P-markers, shown in the derived P-markers of Diagrams 3.16 and 3.17, which results from de-letions clearly goes beyond even that which is produced by order-changing transformations. For example, in Diagram 3.16, not only is there no

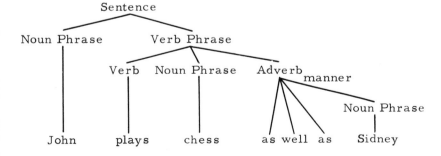

Diagram 3.17

representation of the fact, understood by any speaker, that a second-person element is the subject of <u>eat</u>, but there is no

representation of a second-person element at all. Similarly, in
Diagram 3.17 there is no representation of the fact that intuitively Sidney is the subject of a Verb Phrase which has the form plays
chess. In cases such as these, it is not only that the syntactic
structure required for deciding which readings amalgamate is
not present (as with order-changing transformations), but also
some of the lexical items needed to bear lexical readings are
absent. Hence, if semantic interpretations for sentences such
as (22) and (23) are obtained by P1 operating on derived P-markers, incorrect semantic interpretations will result.

Of course, it might be possible to have P1 operate on derived
P-markers of sentences derived by deletion transformations and
still avoid this result. This could be done by adding otherwise
unmotivated projection rules to the semantic component. For
example, in the case of (22) there might be a 'rule' which says
something like:

1. When the first element in a derived P-marker is an un-
    inflected verb, this P-marker is to be treated semanti-
    cally as if it had a second-person Noun Phrase subject
    and an auxiliary containing will.

Similarly, in the case of (23) there might be a 'rule':

2. When there is a derived P-marker of the form (Noun
    Phrase$_1$ + Verb Phrase$_1$ + as + well + as + Noun Phrase$_2$),
    it is to be treated semantically as if it were of the form:
    (Noun Phrase$_1$ + Verb Phrase$_1$ + as + well + as + Noun
    Phrase$_2$ + Verb Phrase$_1$).

Besides the enormous conceptual difficulties involved in making
'rules' like 1 and 2 precise and in integrating them with the
rest of the semantic component, there is also the enormous, unnecessary complication of having one such special rule for each
different deletion transformation in every language. This would
represent a staggering addition in the complexity of semantic
components, quite independent of the unmotivated complexity and
ad hoc quality of the 'rules' themselves.

The crucial point, however, is that putative projection 'rules'
like 1 and 2 are nothing more than a pointless way of attempt-
ing to reconstruct from derived P-markers the syntactic structure and lexical content that are in fact found in underlying P-
markers but are absent in derived ones. Everything that such
ad hoc 'rules' attempt to do is achieved by having P1 operate
on the underlying P-markers of sentences like (22) and (23) and
similarly in all other cases of deletions.

Finally, let us consider the case of sentences resulting from
adjunction or addition transformations. The chief fact here is
that the elements added by these singulary transformations con-

tribute no meaning to the sentences containing them. Consider
the sentence

(28) John does not go home

In (28) do is just a device to bear the Present Tense morpheme
(es). Thus (28) is just the simple negation of

(29) John goes home

which contains no occurrence of do, and a paraphrase of

(30) it is not the case that John goes home

The semantic difference between (28) and (29) is fully accounted
for by the semantic information associated with not. Support for
this comes from the fact that the string which results from (28)
by deleting do, namely

(31) *John not go home

sounds like a Hollywood version of a foreigner's attempt to speak
English, but it is nevertheless understood uniquely to mean exactly what (28) means. If do actually had meaning, (31) would
differ in meaning from (28). In cases like (28) do is introduced by
a late obligatory transformation in certain cases when the tense
markers of the Auxiliary constituent are separated by intrusive
elements from the following Verb.[13] But the fact that transformations sometimes introduce meaningless elements is another
strong argument for the view that P1 operate on underlying P-
markers. For this condition automatically ensures that these
meaningless elements are never present in P-markers which
are to be semantically interpreted. This makes it unnecessary
to associate null semantic dictionary entries with elements like
do, which would be required if meaningless elements are present
in P-markers which are to be semantically interpreted.[14]
    We have seen that there are a number of conclusive arguments
showing that P1 must operate on underlying P-markers in sentences derived without generalized transformations. In fact,
these arguments show more. They demonstrate that P1 should
apply only to underlying P-markers. If P1 cannot in general
operate on the derived P-markers produced by singular transformations, and if all the information required for the operation
of P1 is found in underlying P-markers, then the most efficient
way to characterize the operation of P1 is simply to require in
such cases that P1 operate on all, and only, the underlying P-
markers. Any attempt to have P1 operate on both underlying
and derived P-markers is pointless because the full interpretation is derivable from the former alone. Such an attempt is ex-
ceedingly complicated in particular cases because the semantic
component must specify exactly which derived P-markers can

be so operated on, for certainly not all can be. Thus the most
empirically adequate and conceptually simple condition which
the general theory of linguistic descriptions can impose on Pl
is that Pl operate exclusively on the underlying P-markers of
sentences derived without the use of generalized transformations.

3.3 Semantic Interpretation of Structures Derived with Generalized Transformations

From the viewpoint of the simplicity of the semantic component as a whole, the best means of providing semantic interpretations for sentences <u>with</u> generalized transformations in their
T-markers is to extend to this case the previous treatment of
sentences <u>without</u> such in their T-markers. If this is possible,
we shall obtain the following uniform and maximally general, and
hence most theoretically adequate, formal means of characterizing the semantic interpretation of all sentences: The meaning of
every sentence is determined uniquely by the operation of projection rules on underlying P-markers. Transformations would
be without semantic effects.

The justification for the position that Pl operate only on the
underlying P-markers of sentences with generalized transformations in their derivational history is exactly the same as that
for the class of sentences derived solely with singulary transformations. Every argument used in Section 3.2 carries over.
This is so because there are sentences, in fact, infinitely many,
whose T-markers contain singulary permutation, deletion, or
adjunction transformations which are applied before the application of generalized transformations.[15] In such cases, the previous application of these structure-distorting transformations
prevents the correct application of Pl on the P-markers they
derive in exactly the same way as in cases without the generalized
transformation, illustrated by sentences like

> (32) I understand that the contestants who play chess as well
> as Sidney have almost all been chosen

Such sentences exhibit quite clearly many of those properties of
derived P-markers which require Pl to operate on underlying
P-markers.

We can draw the same conclusion for sentences derived by
generalized transformations even when no significant singulary
transformations have been applied in the derivation of the Constituent P-marker, because of the facts concerning grammatical
relations. Thus in

> (33) I saw the man who reads comic books

it is necessary to have the projection rules apply to the underlying P-markers because in the otherwise motivated derived

P-marker for (33) there is no information to represent the fact,
required by the Pl, that <u>the man</u> is the grammatical subject of
<u>reads comic books</u>. But if <u>this</u> fact is not made available to
Pl in the <u>normal</u> manner, much <u>ad hoc</u> conceptual machinery
must be added to obtain it in a bizarre manner. The same conclusion holds for other grammatical relations in similar cases.
In a transformational grammar, however, sentences like (33)
are derived from a pair of underlying P-markers. One of these
P-markers has as its last line the string <u>wh the man Present</u>
<u>read comic book Plural</u>. In this P-marker the fact that <u>the man</u>
is the subject of <u>reads comic books</u> is formally represented by
the same devices that express such facts for strings which become full sentences like

(34) the man reads comic books

rather than embedded phrases, namely the configurational technique discussed above.

However, the generalization that the semantic interpretation
of every sentence is uniquely determined by the operation of projection rules on its underlying P-markers has different implications for sentences derived with generalized transformations
and those derived without them. For the latter kind, this generalization is completely represented by the condition that Pl apply
only to underlying P-markers. For the former kind, however,
while this condition is necessary, it is not sufficient to specify
fully the operation of the semantic component. This follows immediately from the fact that sentences derived with generalized
transformations have more than one underlying P-marker. Under
the conditions we have accepted for Pl, each of these P-markers
will receive a semantic interpretation. But it is obviously necessary to provide one single interpretation for the sentence as
a whole, and as yet there is no device for accomplishing this.
This problem does not arise in sentences derived exclusively
with singulary transformations, because such sentences have
only a single underlying P-marker, whose semantic interpretation can be taken as the semantic interpretation of the sentence
as a whole. These considerations make it necessary to introduce
another type of projection rule, in fact the only P2 which we claim
is required by an adequate semantic component. This P2 will
provide a means for combining the separate semantic interpretations of the set of underlying P-markers of a sentoid derived
with generalized transformations into a single semantic interpretation for the sentence as a whole.

Before the P2 can be stated precisely, it is necessary to describe our conception of the operation of generalized transformations. The account will deal only with <u>embedding transforma-</u>
<u>tions</u>. We assume that it can be extended without essential modi-
fication to conjunction transformations.

Thus it is necessary to formulate some of the universal properties of the embedding transformations of any syntactic component.
These formulations should be regarded as part of the general
theory of linguistic descriptions. As so far developed in the work
of Chomsky, this theory characterizes embedding transformations
as those which operate on a pair of P-markers and produce a single, new, derived P-marker by embedding part of one of the orig-
inals in the other. That P-marker which has a subpart embedded
in it is referred to as the Matrix P-marker; that which provides
the part (which need not be a proper part) to be embedded in the
Matrix P-marker is called the Constituent P-marker. We seek
now to formulate this notion of embedding transformation more
fully by adding the following stipulations. We claim that all Matrix P-markers will be characterized by the presence of one or
more specified dummy elements in their last lines. A dummy
element is a morpheme which necessarily never occurs in any
sentence (i.e., is never a formative). There will be at least
two types of dummy elements which are universally found in the
terminal strings of the underlying P-markers of all languages.
The first type is found only in Matrix P-markers and will henceforth be referred to as Matrix dummies (md). The second type
is of no concern here and so will be discussed later. We further
specify the notion of embedding transformation by requiring that
each operate by substituting the Constitutent P-marker for some
occurrence of md.

We specify further that all syntactic components contain among
the nonterminal symbols of their phrase structure subpart a specified set of constituents including at least two, called Relative
(Rel) and Complement (Comp). Each of these constituents is
developed into an occurrence of md as its terminal representative. In other words, besides assuming a certain universal grammatical vocabulary, we assume also a certain set of universal
phrase structure rules. We claim that the grammars of all languages introduce elements like Rel and Comp as subparts of the
major constituents like Noun Phrase, Verb Phrase, etc. In other
words, elements like Noun Phrase and Verb Phrase will dominate,
among other things, sequences of universal elements like Rel
and Comp plus the lexical head constituents of these major categories, i.e., elements like Noun and Verb. In fact, it is quite
likely that Rel and Comp can be identified as a single 'Complement' constituent and that each of a certain set of constituents
dominates such a 'complement' which serves to provide the basis
for recursive expansions. What we are calling 'Rel' is then simply the 'complement' of the Determiner constituent. We shall
not, however, make this identification here.

In terms of the notions described above, we can now specify
that embedding transformations are of two types at most. Many

have the function of substituting the Constituent P-marker for
the md representative of elements like Rel and Comp. It is possible that all embedding transformations have just this function.
However, we leave open the possibility that some embeddings
substitute the Constituent P-marker for md representatives of
the heads of the major categories, i.e., for md representatives
of elements like Noun, Verb, etc. We shall nevertheless see
that a number of cases which appear to have a natural treatment
in these latter terms are in fact best handled by substitutions for
the md representatives of Rel and Comp.

Embeddings which substitute Constituent P-markers for the
md representatives of Rel and Comp provide recursive expansions of the finite number of major constituents like Noun Phrase
and Verb Phrase in underlying P-markers. Thus, for example,
besides the finite number of the Noun Phrase in English, like the
book, substitutions for the md representative of Rel produce a
boundless number of other Noun Phrases like

(35)   the book which was taken by the man who Mary saw on
       her way to the red school

The treatment of Rel and Comp described earlier is dictated
by a number of syntactic motivations, including especially considerations of derived constituent structure and simplicity. The
latter relate particularly to the fact that it is often necessary to
refer to the embedded or derived element produced by an embedding transformation as a whole after the embedding. The fact
that there are single nodes like Rel dominating all such cases
permits this to be done in the simplest manner. Having all embeddings substitute the Constituent P-marker for an md greatly
simplifies the rules of derived constituent structure, since the
substituent here simply takes on the structure of the dummy it
replaces. Finally, the fact that every Matrix P-marker is characterized by the presence of at least one md permits a simple
formal specification of the set of Matrix P-markers, a specification required to state which sequences of transformations produce permissible derivations.

Although the universality of Rel and Comp is not necessarily
required on semantic grounds, it has strong syntactic motivation. Instances of Rel and Comp in the phrase structure derivations of a syntactic component must be developed into an occurrence of md.[16] Many ad hoc rules would be required if each syntactic component had to specify the constituency of Rel and Comp
like elements individually.

From the preceding account of the way in which generalized
transformations combine a Constituent P-marker with a Matrix
P-marker, it is clear that P2 must somehow provide a semantic
analogue for this syntactic process. However, formulating this

analogue is not as simple as it might first appear. It is not just
a matter of associating some part of the semantic interpretation
of the Constituent P-marker with the semantic interpretation of
the Matrix P-marker, because in most (perhaps all) cases the
P-markers combined by generalized transformations are not them
selves underlying P-markers and thus receive no interpretations
from the operation of P1. This is so because singulary transformations may derive both Matrix and Constituent P-markers
for embedding transformations and, most importantly, because
the P-markers which undergo embedding transformations may
themselves result from previous applications of embedding transformations, and so on, without bound. Indeed, this latter possibility is just the provision made by a transformational syntactic
component for non-co-ordinational recursion. It is clear, therefore, that P2 cannot operate on the actual P-markers which are
combined in the operations of embedding transformations since
these are in general derived rather than underlying P-markers.
    Schematically, we can describe the situations in which P2 must
operate as in Diagram 3.18, assuming for the sake of simplicity (contrary to fact) that each P-marker contains at most one
occurrence of md. Diagram 3.18 represents two fundamental
facts: first, that a single sentoid may have arbitrarily many
underlying P-markers; and second, that the final derived P-
marker of a sentoid results from successively embedding P-
markers in each other. This recursive process builds up more
and more complex P-markers by embedding complex P-markers
in simple P-markers to produce still more complex P-markers.
In Diagram 3.18, triangles represent P-markers, and rectangles
represent transformations. The symbols UP and DP distinguish,
respectively, underlying and derived P-markers. Rectangles
containing the symbol T_s represent arbitrary finite sequences
of singulary transformations. Rectangles containing the symbol T_g represent an arbitrary single generalized transformation.
The diagram thus represents the fact that each member of a pair
of underlying P-markers may undergo a finite (perhaps null) set
of singulary transformations to yield a pair of new derived P-
markers. This pair may then undergo a generalized transformation which embeds one in the other to derive a single new derived
P-marker. The latter may then undergo a finite sequence of singulary transformations, producing a single P-marker as output.
And this output may, by another application of some generalized
transformation, be embedded in a P-marker which results from
the application of a finite set of singulary transformations on
some other underlying P-marker, etc. The three dots in the
middle of Diagram 3.18 indicate that there is no bound on the
number of such successive embeddings. Each underlying P-
marker, except the last, UP_1, must contain at least one occur-

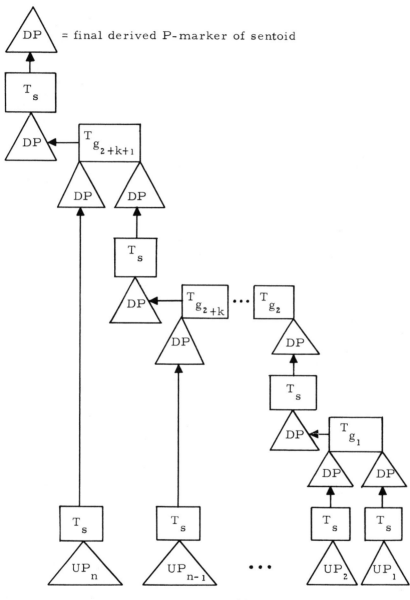

Diagram 3.18

rence of an md. These dummy occurrences will also appear in
the P-markers which result from the application of singulary
transformations, and the md are not removed until they are replaced by a Constituent P-marker by means of the operation of
some embedding transformation.

Consider now the problem of semantically interpreting sentoids whose SD are represented by structures like Diagram 3.18. Since P1 operate on underlying P-markers, they will operate on UP_1, ..., UP_n in Diagram 3.18, i.e., on every underlying P-marker in the SD. The P-marker UP_1 will be fully interpreted by P1. But in P-markers UP_2, ..., UP_n the P1 will be <u>blocked</u> at every point where it would be necessary to combine some reading with that of an md, since these dummy elements have no readings. Since P1 require readings to operate on, prior to the application of P2, P1 will provide no set of derived readings for any constituent that dominates an md. In particular, therefore, P1 will provide no derived readings for the 'Sentence' constituents of any underlying P-markers whose terminal strings contain occurrences of md. Therefore P1 provide only a <u>partial</u> semantic interpretation for any underlying P-marker containing an occurrence of md but <u>full</u> interpretations for underlying P-markers without such dummies. It is at this point, where the operation of P1 is blocked, that the operation of P2 is required.

The situation of embedding with which Diagram 3.18 starts is shown in Diagram 3.19. In this diagram, the underlying P-marker UP_1 necessarily contains no occurrence of md and is thus fully interpreted by P1 alone. Since UP_2 necessarily contains an occurrence of md, it is only partially interpreted. Diagram 3.19 represents one full embedding. This might in itself be the full SD of some sentoid, or it might be only the first step in the derivation of a sentoid containing more than one embedding. In either case, the task of the P2 can be characterized as that of providing a set of derived readings for the constituent that immediately dominates the occurrence of md in UP_2 on the basis of the readings assigned by P1 to UP_1. In other words, the semantic analogue of the syntactic process of embedding is, we claim, the association of the readings from the underlying P-markers which are the bases for the Constituent P-marker of the embedding with a constituent in the underlying P-marker which is the basis for the Matrix P-marker of the embedding. An underlying P-marker is the basis for another derived P-marker if the latter is derived from the former by the successive application of a set of singulary transformations. A set of

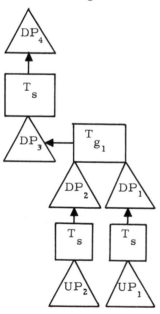

Diagram 3.19

underlying P-markers is the basis for some derived P-marker
if the latter is derived from the former by the successive application of generalized and singular transformations. This constituent with which the readings are associated is that one which
immediately dominates the occurrence of md, such as Rel and
Comp. Hence, in Diagram 3.19 the P2 will associate each Sentence
reading from the full semantic interpretation of UP_1 (produced
by P1) with the constituent in UP_2 that immediately dominates
the occurrence of md. As shown, UP_1 and UP_2 are, respectively,
the bases for DP_1 and DP_2, which are the P-markers actually
combined by the generalized transformation.

The operation of P2, however, is not restricted to the case
depicted in Diagram 3.19 where the SD of a sentoid contains only
one embedding, nor to the first embedding in a SD containing more
than one. Diagram 3.20 depicts the situation where P2 must apply to an embedding which is not the first. For the case depicted

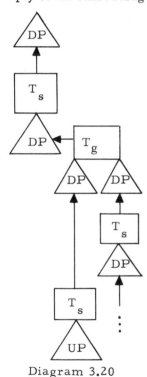

in Diagram 3.20, the task of P2 is to provide a set of derived readings for the constituent that immediately dominates md
in the underlying P-marker, which is the
basis for the Matrix of the embedding, in
terms of readings assigned by P1 to the n
bases of the Constituent P-marker of the
embedding and by previous applications of
P2. Because of the similarities between
the cases in Diagram 3.19 and 3.20, we can
abstractly characterize the task of P2 in
such a way as to cover both of these cases.
Such a characterization enables us to achieve
the maximum generality in the formulation
of P2. Thus, given an arbitrary embedding,
P2 associates the set of readings assigned
to the 'Sentence' nodes of the nth underlying P-marker of the set of underlying P-
markers (which are the bases for the Constituent P-marker of the embedding) with
that constituent immediately dominating the
occurrence of md in the underlying P-marker (which is the basis for the Matrix P-
marker of the embedding). After the ap-

Diagram 3.20

plication of the P2 to an underlying P-mark-
er which is the basis for some Matrix P-marker, the operation
of P1 is no longer blocked in that underlying P-marker. Now,
in the positions where md occur, readings have been inserted,
namely those from the 'Sentence' constituent of the nth underlying P-marker of the bases of the Constituent P-marker of the
embedding. Thus, those P1 which are relevant perform the

amalgamations necessary to provide a full semantic interpretation for the basis of the Matrix P-marker. This process of un-
blocking begins with the basis of the Matrix P-marker of the
first embedding and proceeds, embedding by embedding, to make
P1 applicable and hence permit the successive semantic interpretation of the basis of each Matrix P-marker.

In this informal characterization of P2, the ordering which
uniquely determines the nth underlying P-marker for a given
embedding is crucial. That some ordering is necessary is in
the nature of the case. In order to have a set of readings to assign the constituent immediately dominating the md in the ith underlying P-marker, it is necessary that there be a set of readings assigned to the 'Sentence' node in the $(i-1)^{th}$ underlying P-
marker. But the more significant fact is that the character of
the ordering is crucial. This is shown most clearly by the fact
that there are distinct sentoids containing exactly the same set
of underlying P-markers. Consider

(36) I know that the boy who John likes hates Mary

(37) the boy who I know that John likes hates Mary

The only independently motivated underlying P-markers for these
sentences are shown in Diagrams 3.21-3.23. The difference between (36) and (37) must be attributed solely to the order in which
the embeddings have taken place.
Sentence (36) results when the
P-marker in Diagram 3.23 is
embedded in that of Diagram
3.22 and the result embedded
in that of Diagram 3.21 (all with
appropriate interspersing of the
application of singular transformations). Sentence (37) results when the P-marker in
Diagram 3.23 is embedded in

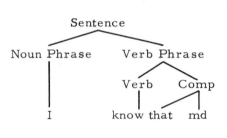

Diagram 3.21

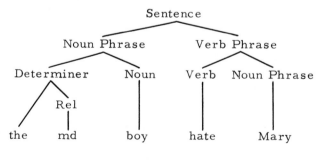

Diagram 3.22

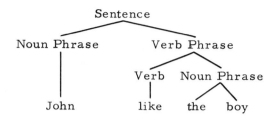

Diagram 3.23

that of Diagram 3.21, the result being embedded in that of Diagram 3.22 (again with appropriate interspersing of singulary
transformation applications). Since we must therefore certainly regard (36) and (37) as being associated with distinct sentoids,
it follows that the SD generated by the syntactic component must
include specification not only of the set of underlying P-markers
and applied transformations (both example sentences involve application of the same transformations, in particular the same
generalized transformations — e. g. , the relative — and one of
the verbal complement transformations) but also of the order in
which transformational operations on underlying and derived P-
markers occur. In fact, we have allowed for this possibility
since we stipulated that the SD of a sentoid must specify not only
the underlying P-markers but also, by means of a T-marker,
the relevant transformational applications. Thus it is necessary
to show how T-markers can provide the kind of ordering necessary to represent successive embeddings in sentoids containing
multiple applications of generalized transformations. We must
therefore characterize precisely the notion of T-marker.

   In order to do this, it will be necessary to digress somewhat.
A sentoid must contain a representation of the transformations
that have been applied in its derivation. A grammar must provide for each level $\underline{L}$ in sentoids a set of L-markers to represent grammatical utterances on that level. The notion of level
can be characterized in terms of the structures generated by
a set of rules of a fixed type. On the levels of a grammar other
than the transformational, the L-markers are sets of strings
of elements under concatenation. For example, on the phonetic
level, the L-markers consist of sets composed of a single string,
a string of phonetic segments. On the level of phrase structure,
the L-markers (underlying P-markers) are sets of strings drawn
from equivalent phrase structure subcomponent derivations, etc.[17]
It is therefore natural and necessary for a homogeneous linguistic theory also to take L-markers on the transformational level
to be sets of strings under concatenation.

   On the transformational level the elements which are to be
concatenated, the 'basic vocabulary' of the level, will consist

of underlying P-markers and the transformations themselves.
Succession of an underlying P-marker and a transformation will
be interpreted to mean the application of that transformation to
that P-marker. Succession of two (singulary) transformations
will be interpreted to mean application of the second to the derived P-marker given as output by the first. The T-marker of
each sentoid could be trivially characterized as a single string
were it not for generalized transformations, for these apply to
pairs of P-markers, each of which may be the result of the operation of an independent sequence of transformations (these sequences including other generalized transformations) on underlying P-markers. Thus generalized transformations give a 'two-
dimensional' aspect or tree structure to the set of transformations applied in the derivation of some (in fact, most) sentoids.
If the numbers 3.21, 3.22, and 3.23 stand for the P-markers
found in the Diagrams 3.21, 3.22, and 3.23, we can illustrate
the two-dimensional tree structure introduced by generalized
transformations in Diagram 3.24, which gives the transformational history of Example (36). Therefore, if T-markers are
to be represented as strings,
it is necessary to represent
this two-dimensional aspect
in one dimension. This can
be done naturally by establishing an arbitrary one-di-
mensional order in the general
theory of linguistic descriptions for the transformations

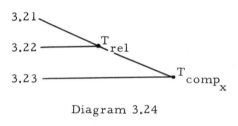

Diagram 3.24

which have yielded the Matrix and Constituent P-markers of embeddings. It can also be done by ordering with these transformations the generalized transformations which map these pairs of
P-markers into single new P-markers.
   We define the following notions:

   A Kernel String (K-string) is any string in the vocabulary
   U$\bar{P}$, T_s, such that its first element is a UP and all its remaining elements are T_s. Thus the general form of a K-
   string is $UP_i + T_{s_1} + \ldots + T_{s_n}$, where UP_i is the designation of some underlying P-marker and $T_{s_1} + \ldots + T_{s_n}$ is
   the designation of some sequence of singulary transformations.

K-strings are to be interpreted to mean that the singulary transformation designated by T_{s_1} applies to the underlying P-marker
UP_i, that the singulary transformation designated by T_{s_2} applies
to the derived P-marker which results from the application of
T_{s_1}, etc.

A Generalized String (G-string) is either a K-string or any string of the form

(a) $K_1 + K_2 + T_g$, where K_1 and K_2 are K-strings

or

(b) $G_1 + G_2 + T_g$, where G_1 and G_2 are G-strings

and where T_g is some generalized transformation.

The intended interpretation of G-strings is as follows. A substring of the form $G_1 + G_2 + T_g$ asserts that T_g embeds the P-marker resulting from the last transformation in G_2 in the P-marker resulting from the last transformation in G_1.

The Transformation Marker (T-marker) of a sentoid is the maximal G-string in the sentoid.[18]

Those familiar with Polish notation in symbolic logic will recognize that this characterization of the notion of transformation marker eliminates the bracketing found in the description of transformational embeddings by the parenthesis-free coding of Polish notation.

We can at once illustrate the notion of T-marker and show how T-markers provide the kind of ordering required by the P2 by considering the alternative T-markers associated with our earlier examples (36) and (37). As previously noted, these contain the same underlying P-markers, those in Diagrams 3.21-3.23 and the same transformations, namely T_{rel} and T_{comp_x} (we ignore singularies as irrelevant here). Abbreviating these underlying P-markers as in Diagram 3.24 and eliminating for simplicity all singulary transformations, we can represent the distinct T-markers of (36) and (37) as follows: Example (36) has associated with it the T-marker shown in Diagram 3.25, while (37) has associated with it the T-marker shown in Diagram 3.26. The bracketing over the strings of UP and T_g is not actually part of the T-marker but is given only to illustrate the structure of the T-markers. These T-markers assert that (36) is the result of embedding 3.23 in 3.22 by T_{rel} and of embedding the result of this in 3.21 by

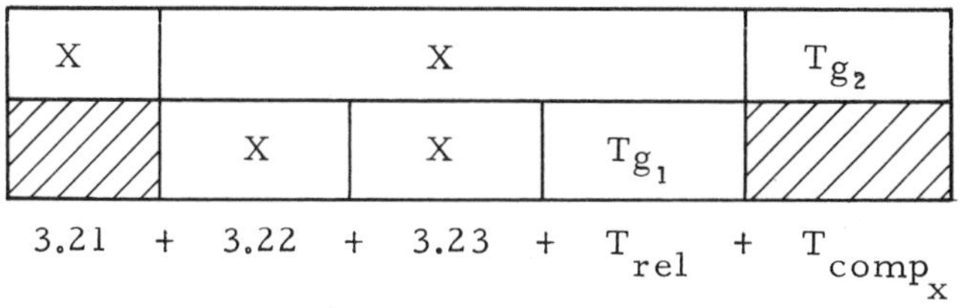

X	X			T_{g_2}
////	X	X	T_{g_1}	////

3.21   +   3.22   +   3.23   + T_{rel} + T_{comp_x}

Diagram 3.25

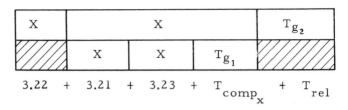

Diagram 3.26

T_{comp_x}, while (37) is the result of embedding 3.23 in 3.21 by T_{comp_x} and of embedding the result of this in 3.22 by T_{rel}. We can thus see how T-markers represent the order of successive embeddings in sentoids containing multiple applications of generalized transformations by linearizing the tree character of transformational history. This is done by specifying that those substrings which underlie the Matrix P-marker are to the left of those which underlie the Constituent P-marker, and that both of these are to the left of the generalized transformation which actually carries out the embedding.

We would now be in a position to state the P2 precisely if it were not for the fact that we have consistently simplified the description of sentoids containing generalized transformations by limiting all P-markers to one occurrence of md. That this restriction has no basis in fact is easily shown by such examples as

(38) the man who is happy likes the man who is sad

The difficulty caused by the need for more than one occurrence of md in a P-marker reaches an extreme form, since the sentoid represented by

(39) the man who is sad likes the man who is happy

contains exactly the same set of underlying P-markers as that represented by (38), namely those shown in Diagrams 3.27-3.29. Despite the fact that (38) and (39) have the same set of underlying P-markers, they must represent distinct sentoids. The question naturally arises whether or not the difference between (38) and (39) can be represented in T-markers by the kind of ordering which differentiates the sentoids of (36) and (37). In this earlier case, we found n underlying P-markers, none containing more than a single occurrence of md and one without any occurrence of md at all, which were successively embedded in one another. In that case, a P-marker PM resulting from an embedding transformation (or the output produced by operation of subsequent singularies on PM) could only serve as the Constituent P-marker of later embeddings. In the present case, how-

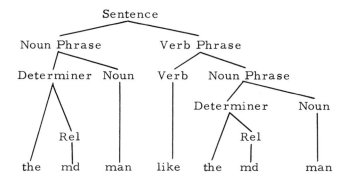

Diagram 3.27

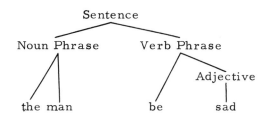

Diagram 3.28

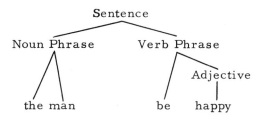

Diagram 3.29

ever, a P-marker PM which is the output of an embedding transformation (or the output produced by operation of singularies on
PM) may serve as the <u>Matrix</u> P-marker for a subsequent embedding because PM (and one of its bases) originally contained more
than one occurrence of md.

Despite this contrast between the two cases, contrasting sentoids for sentences like (38) and (39) can in fact be distinguished
in terms of the ordering found in T-markers. Our previous interpretative principle specified that a particular generalized
transformation was to embed a certain Constituent P-marker in
a specified Matrix P-marker. However, this principle is precise
only if the occurrence of the md which is to be replaced in each

Matrix P-marker is somehow uniquely specified. Previously
we introduced the fiction that each Matrix contained exactly one
occurrence of md. This fiction enabled us to specify uniquely
the occurrence of md which was to be replaced by an embedding.
This fiction must be dispensed with, but at the same time the requirement of unique specification for the md to be replaced by a
particular embedding must be maintained. For if this requirement is not met, the interpretative principle for T-markers does
not specify where the Constituent P-marker is to be embedded
and thus does not guarantee a unique output of derived P-markers for sentoids, i.e., does not uniquely associate terminal
strings of formatives with their SD.

  We add to our characterization of the transformational subcomponent the following two conditions:

  (i)   In an embedding, the Constituent P-marker is inserted
        at the point of the leftmost occurrence of md in the
        Matrix P-marker.[19]

  (ii) If any P-marker PM contains an occurrence of md, then
        PM cannot, for this reason, be the Constituent P-mark-
        er of an embedding.

Condition (i) determines an ordering of the occurrences of md
in Matrix P-markers which makes possible an unique association
of each Constituent P-marker with the md which it replaces.

  The T-markers are formal objects whose elements are underlying P-markers and the designations of transformations. The
interpretative principle for T-markers (given earlier) is such
that the set of T-markers uniquely characterizes the set of all
possible transformational derivations. Thus (i) and (ii) are conditions, not on T-markers themselves, but on the derivations
that these determine. These conditions impose restrictions on
the generative mechanism G (cf. note 18) which determines the
set of T-markers; i.e., G must be such that the set of T-markers which it generates yields (by our interpretative principle)
only transformational derivations which meet Conditions (i) and
(ii). However, nothing in the characterization of T-markers as
such guarantees that the element X_2 in configurations of the form
$X_1 + X_2 + T_g$ is such that its output P-marker contains no occurrences of md, and hence that this output P-marker can be a Constituent P-marker which T_g embeds in the output P-marker of
X_1. Both (i) and (ii) provide just this guarantee. Condition (ii)
guarantees that no P-marker which is the final output of an X_2
can be embedded unless it is free of occurrences of md. In effect, it says that after a P-marker is embedded in another P-
marker, nothing may be embedded in the former. Condition (i)
provides an ordering for embeddings that specifies the manner

in which transformations successively eliminate occurrences of
md. If it is assumed that P-markers can contain more than one
occurrence of md, it is (ii) which guarantees that the order of
underlying P-markers and transformations such as those shown
in Diagram 3.18 and represented formally in T-markers determines a unique order of successive embedding.[20]
The difference between (38) and (39) and all analogous cases
is specifiable by stating which Constituent P-marker is embedded
where. According to the conditions on transformational derivations just introduced, the ordering of elements in T-markers can
distinguish such cases directly. If the underlying P-markers of
(38) and (39) are abbreviated by the numbers of their diagrams,
and if all singular transformations are eliminated for simplicity,
then (38) and (39) have respectively the following T-markers:

$$3.27 + 3.29 + T_{rel} + 3.28 + T_{rel}; \quad 3.27 + 3.28 + T_{rel} + 3.29 + T_{rel}$$

According to our interpretative principle for T-markers and
Conditions (i) and (ii), these T-markers tell us that (38) is
formed by first embedding 3.29 at the point of the leftmost occurrence of md in 3.27 and subsequently embedding 3.28 in the
result of this; and that (39) is derived by first embedding 3.28
in 3.27 at the point of the leftmost occurrence of md and subsequently embedding 3.29 in the result of the first embedding.
Having shown how T-markers can formally represent both the
order of successive embeddings and the points at which embeddings occur, we are ready to state the P2. Preparatory to this
we must define the following notion:

Successive Embedding Basis (SEB). Let

$$\alpha + Z + T_{g_1} + \ldots + T_{g_n} + \beta$$

be an arbitrary T-marker such that
   (1) Z contains no T_g
   (2) α is either null or has a T_g as its rightmost element
   (3) β is either null or has an underlying P-marker as its
        leftmost element

An SEB is the sequence of underlying P-markers in Z. An SEB
is also a formal representation of the maximal set of underlying P-markers which are combined to form a structure to be inserted for a single occurrence of md in some P-marker. The
definition takes advantage of the fact that in a T-marker occurrences of T_g followed by underlying P-markers indicate that
some preceding underlying P-marker contains more than one
occurrence of md. Consider Diagram 3.30, which represents
two contrasting T-markers. In (I) there are two SEB, 1 + 2
and 3 + 4, while in (II) there is only a single SEB, namely
1 + 2 + 3 + 4. Thus in (I) there is first derived a pair of complex

(I)
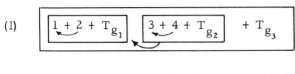

where 1, 2, 3, 4 are
each underlying P-markers

(II)
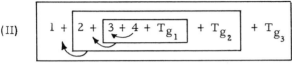

Diagram 3.30

structures, one by embedding 2 in 1, the other by embedding 4
in 3; the final result is obtained by embedding the result of the
latter in that of the former. The two SEB's thus represent the
fact that this sentence involves an underlying P-marker with multiple occurrences of md, namely 1. In (II), 4 is embedded in 3,
the result of this in 2, and the result of this in 1. No P-marker
contains more than one md.

The set of underlying P-markers in the T-marker of a sentoid
is initially operated on by P1. Every underlying P-marker in
the set which contains no occurrence of md will be fully interpreted; i.e., each of its constituents will be assigned a set of
readings. But as noted earlier, no constituent which dominates
an occurrence of md will receive a set of readings because the
P1 are blocked when they reach the point in a P-marker where
an md occurs. We can now state the P2, completing the assignment of a set of readings to each constituent of underlying P-
markers containing occurrences of md. We define P2 as follows:

> Begin with the SEB's. Each SEB is of the form UP_1, UP_2,
> ..., UP_n, where n > 1. Starting with the rightmost pair
> in the SEB, UP_{n-1} and UP_n, and taking the pairs successively,
> assign the set of readings associated with the node 'Sentence'
> in UP_i to the constituent immediately dominating the left-
> most occurrence of md in UP_{i-1} whose immediately dominat-
> ing constituent has no set of readings already assigned to it.
> Then, for the sequence of SEB's where m > 1, SEB_1, SEB_2,
> ..., SEB_m, starting with the rightmost pair, SEB_{m-1} and
> SEB_m, and taking these pairs successively, assign the set
> of readings associated with the node 'Sentence' in the left-
> most P-marker of SEB_i to the constituent immediately dom-
> inating the leftmost occurrence of md whose immediately
> dominating constituent has no set of readings already as-
> signed to it in the leftmost P-marker of SEB_{i-1}.

Since P1 operate wherever they are applicable, P1 operate prior
to every assignment of a set of readings by P2. Before a set of
readings is assigned to the constituent immediately dominating

the leftmost occurrence of md in UP_{i-2}, the P1 operate to make all the amalgamations they can in UP_{i-1}. Likewise, before a set of readings is assigned to the constituent immediately domi- nating the leftmost P-marker of SEB_{i-2}, the P1 operate to make all the amalgamations they can in the leftmost P-marker of SEB_{i-1}. Thus the applications of P2 unblock the process of assigning read- ings to constituents by P1 by successively providing readings at specified points in underlying P-markers which originally received only partial interpretations from P1.

We can illustrate the operation of the P2 by considering how it would interpret the sentoids associated with the sets of contrast- ing sentences (36) and (37), and (38) and (39). In the former case, the P1 would apply to the underlying P-markers in Diagrams 3.21- 3.23. A full interpretation would be provided for P-marker 3.23 but only partial interpretations for 3.21 and 3.22. Then the P2 would apply to the SEB of the T-marker for (36), namely 3.21 + 3.22 + 3.23, and would insert the set of readings associated with Sentence in 3.23 with the Rel constituent in 3.22. Next, the P1 would apply to 3.22 and finish its interpretation. Then, the P2 would reapply and assign the set of readings associated with the node Sentence in 3.22 with the constituent Comp in 3.21. Finally, the P1 would reapply and finish the interpretation of 3.21. The set of readings assigned to the node Sentence in 3.21 is the one for Ex- ample (36) as a whole. The interpretation of (37) would proceed anal- ogously by utilizing its SEB instead, namely 3.22 + 3.21 + 3.23.

For the contrasting sentences (38) and (39) the situation is some- what more complicated. These have the underlying P-markers found in Diagrams 3.27-3.29, but their T-markers (Diagram 3.30) provide each with two SEB's. Consider (38), which has the SEB 3.27 + 3.29 and null + 3.28. The P1 operate on all of the under- lying P-markers 3.27-3.29 and fully interpret 3.28 and 3.29 but only partially interpret 3.27. The P2 does not apply to the first SEB, null + 3.28, because its first element is null, thus failing the requirement of $n > 1$. The P2 does apply to the second SEB, 3.27 + 3.29, and inserts the set of readings associated with S in 3.29 at the leftmost Rel in 3.27. Then the P1 reapply to 3.27 and fully interpret it. Next, the P2 reapplies to the sequence of two SEB's and inserts the set of readings associated with Sentence in 3.28 at the second (or rightmost) Rel in 3.27. Finally, the P1 re- apply to 3.27 and finish its interpretation. The set of readings as- sociated with Sentence in 3.27 at the end of all projection rule ap- plications provides the interpretation for (38) as a whole. The interpretation of (39) proceeds analogously, utilizing its distinct pair of SEB's. It is important that within this conception of pro- jection rules, the set of readings for a sentence S_i as a whole is the set finally assigned to the node Sentence in the leftmost under- lying P-marker in the entire T-marker of S_i.

There is no reason to require that Pl be ordered in terms of
priority of application with respect either to each other or to P2.
The set of projection rules of a semantic component is thus an
unordered set. Each rule applies when the conditions of its application are met, and no two rules apply in the same case because no two rules have the same conditions of application.

3.4 Readings for Constituents

In Section 2.2, it was noted that an important requirement on
the adequacy of a semantic component is that not only must every
whole sentence receive a set of readings but every constituent
of each sentence must receive a set of readings. This requirement is somewhat vague since the notion of constituent is relative to a particular P-marker and, as we have seen, all sentences have more than one P-marker and most have many more.
It is clear that the theory presented earlier guarantees that every
constituent in every underlying P-marker receives a set of readings. But the semantic component was designed in such a way
that in the case of SD containing generalized transformations,
P2 transfers successively only the readings associated with nodes
labeled 'Sentence'. Thus in such SD a set of readings for many of
the constituents of underlying P-markers cannot be obtained from
the final, semantically interpreted underlying P-marker (the leftmost in the T-marker), but rather must be obtained by considering the readings of the constituents in all the underlying P-markers.

Hence, the reading for a Main Verb consititutent like

(40) are attractive

in a sentence such as

(41) I saw the boy who likes girls who are attractive

is not represented in the leftmost semantically interpreted underlying P-marker of (41), which is shown in Diagram 3.31, but
rather in another of the underlying P-markers of (41), which is
shown in Diagram 3.32. The string of morphemes in (40) is actually represented in the underlying P-marker of Diagram 3.32
(in slightly different order). Yet some of the strings of sentences
like (41) which are derived by generalized transformation require sets of readings even though they are not actually found in
any underlying P-marker. For example, the string

(42) girls who are attractive

requires a reading, in (41), and yet this string of morphemes
(girl + Plural + wh + girl + Plural + be + Present + attractive)
is found in neither Diagram 3.31, 3.32, nor 3.33, which is the
leftmost underlying P-marker in the T-marker of (41).

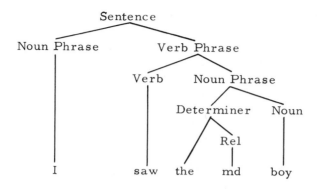

Diagram 3.31

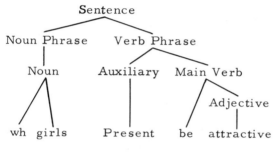

Diagram 3.32

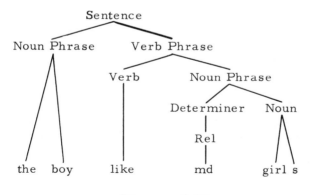

Diagram 3.33

The string in Example (42) is found only in one of the derived P-markers produced by transformations (including embeddings). Yet the present theory of projection rules, which provides semantic interpretations only for the constituents of underlying P-mark-

ers, does, in fact, automatically provide readings for strings
like (42).

It is necessary to say only that the reading for (42) is just the
reading of the structure underlying (42). In this case the reading for (42) is the full reading for the rightmost Noun Phrase constituent in the underlying P-marker of Diagram 3.33. This reading is provided by P1 after the P2 assigns the Sentence reading of
Diagram 3.32 to the Rel in Diagram 3.33. Thus, in general, the
appropriate readings for all strings, both those found in underlying and those found in derived P-markers, regardless of whether
or not the SD contains generalized transformations, are represented by the present theory of projection rules, which permits
the semantic interpretation of only underlying P-markers. All
appropriate readings are exhausted by the set of readings found
on the full set of semantically interpreted underlying P-markers.

3.5 The Formalization of the Restriction of Projection Rules to Underlying P-markers

Since the application of projection rules must be restricted to
underlying P-markers, a natural way of building this restriction
into the internal structure of the semantic component must be
found. The simplest way of doing this is to have semantic information from the dictionary assigned only to the occurrences of
lexical items in underlying P-markers. Since transformations
do not add any lexical items, derived P-markers can contain no
new lexical items, and so the set of lexical items in the underlying P-markers of a sentoid is exhaustive. Moreover, if sets
of readings from the dictionary are never associated with occurrences of lexical items in derived P-markers, no P1 can operate on any derived P-marker. According to the previous formulation of P2, no readings are carried over from an underlying
P-marker to a derived P-marker. Therefore, it follows that
no derived P-marker is ever semantically interpreted by a semantic component. For this reason, the principle which takes
semantic information from the dictionary and associates it with
lexical items in underlying P-markers — the analogue of rule
(i) of earlier papers[21] and above (p. 18) — must be formulated so
that it associates such information only with elements in underlying P-markers.

3.6 Application to Definitions of Semantic Properties of Sentences

Where the value of C is Sentence, the definitions of semantic
properties given in Section 2.2 are equivocal for any sentoid
that has a generalized transformation in its T-marker. They
are unequivocal in the case of sentoids with only singulary
transformations in their T-marker, because only the underlying P-marker of such sentoids is semantically interpreted.
But in the former case, there is always more than one se-

mantically interpreted P-marker. This raises the question as
to which of the semantically interpreted P-markers the variable PM in the definiens of definitions (D1) through (D5) in
Chapter 2 and other such definitions refers to. We can now
use the foregoing formulation of P2 to render these definitions
unequivocal. We simply stipulate that the variable PM in such
definitions be a variable over only the leftmost underlying P-
marker in T-markers of sentoids, where the value of C is Sentence.

3.7 A Way of Eliminating P2

An alternative conception of the syntactic component, which is
presently being developed,[22] would eliminate generalized transformations from the syntactic component in favor of a single substitution rule for combining underlying P-markers. This rule
would combine a pair of underlying P-markers by substituting
one entire underlying P-marker for an occurrence of md in the
other just in case this pair satisfies a compatibility condition
which is, in effect, the equivalent of the structure index of a
generalized transformation. The result of any such combination is a compound P-marker. The maximal such compound P-
marker in a sentoid is singled out and referred to as the generalized P-marker of the sentoid. The generalized P-marker is
the formal object upon which the singulary transformations operate, and thus derived P-markers are the result of applying
singulary transformations to generalized P-markers. Several
facts suggest that this alternative is preferable to the present
conception on purely syntactic grounds, but we cannot consider
these facts here.

It is evident that the full semantic interpretation of a sentoid
can be obtained by the operation of P1 on generalized P-markers
exclusively. Hence, if the syntactic component is formulated in
accord with this alternative conception, the semantic component
requires no P2. The reason that the present conception of linguistic descriptions does require a P2 in semantic components
is that the method which the present conception specifies for
combining P-markers, namely generalized transformations,
does not combine only underlying P-markers; rather, generalized
transformations produce P-markers whose structure is highly
distorted, from the viewpoint of underlying P-markers and semantic interpretation.

The possibility of such an alternative clearly displays the real
function of P2. Such a projection rule serves, in effect, to make
up in the semantic component for the failure of the syntactic component to provide a single formal object capable of being semantically interpreted by P1.

It should be emphasized that, regardless of whether or not this
major modification of the syntactic component is found to be cor-

rect, the major claim of this monograph remains unaffected. The
projection rules of the semantic component operate exclusively
on the structure provided by underlying P-markers and their combinations. However, if this alternative conception of the syntactic component is accepted, we can achieve a fully uniform and
simpler characterization of the notion 'projection rule', since
all projection rules then are P1.

NOTES

1. Klima (1964) and Lees (1960).

2. Chomsky (1957) and Lees (1960).

3. It is of course always possible to provide some kind of simi-
    larity in an ad hoc way. For example, one could arbitrarily
    recognize a node Subject dominating the appropriate elements
    in contrast to another node Object. But this is of no explana-
    tory value, for no independent grammatical motivations can
    be found for introducing such nodes into the syntactic descrip-
    tion.

4. The presence of the pronoun forms in these P-markers is
    discussed in greater detail below, as are the constituent Nu-
    cleus and the morpheme Q.

5. Chomsky (1964 b).

6. The md symbols here are Matrix dummies replaced by em-
    bedding transformations. This process is described and
    justified in detail on page 48.

7. This 'distortion' cannot in any way be considered simply a
    defect of transformation grammars, because the 'distorted'
    structures which result from transformations are the only
    kinds of structure recognized by nontransformational ap-
    proaches to syntax. That is, these approaches recognize
    only various types of segmentation and classification of the
    actual strings of words found in sentences, the final derived
    P-markers of transformational grammars. Transformation-
    al grammars represent this structure plus additional kinds
    of abstract ones.

8. Even if this ad hoc course is taken, the condition of empiri-
    cal adequacy would still not be met, since there would be no
    way of ensuring a correct reading for every constituent. In
    (16), for example, there is no way of ensuring that the Verb
    constituent gets the full reading of look up.

9. There is apparently a psychological (but nongrammatical)
    tendency to avoid the use of complex phrases between discon-

tinuous elements, particularly where <u>complex</u> means 'derived
by generalized transformation'. For a discussion, cf. Chomsky (1961).

10. Cf. Chomsky (1957, 1962).

11. The fact that some derivations of discontinuities are obligatory (such as that in <u>he looked it up</u>) does not affect this generalization. Obviously, these cases also receive the correct
treatment under our conception of the way P1 operate.

12. We note later that this is a simplification in the case of Example (22).

13. Cf. Chomsky (1957), p. 113.

14. Since elements with <u>no</u> readings block the operation of
P1.

15. These applications are very probably restricted to the derivation of the Constituent P-marker, and may not apply to the
Matrix P-marker. For this distinction, cf. Lees (1960) and
our discussion on page 48. For the motivations for this type
of restriction on the interrelations between generalized and
singulary transformations, cf. Fillmore (1963).

16. We do not mean to exclude the possibility that Rel and Comp
are first developed into the intermediate constituents, e.g.,
Rel into $Rel_{appositive}$ and $Rel_{restrictive}$, these intermediate constituents then being developed into occurrences of
md.

17. Cf. Chomsky (1955) for discussion of levels, markers, etc.

18. The set of underlying P-markers which occurs in the sentoids of a language is fully determined by the set of phrase
structure rules. But it is, of course, crucial to be able to
determine as well the set of all <u>T-markers</u> since this set
determines the set of sentoids. What has to be said, either
in general linguistic theory or in individual grammars, about
the relations between individual transformations in order to
determine correctly the (infinite) set of all T-markers? This
is the question discussed by Lees [(1960) pp. 57-59] under
the rubric of 'traffic rules'. This question is equivalent to
asking for specification of the generative mechanism G which
generates the set of T-markers. There are three distinct
positions which might be taken on this subject. First, it
might be maintained that the set of all T-markers is determined by simply applying all transformations in all possible
orders, and applying each whenever it is applicable. This
position assumes that any possible restrictions among transformations are <u>correctly</u> built into the structure indices of

these transformations and that nothing further need be said
either in individual grammars or in general linguistic theory.
It has been apparent almost from the beginning of work on
transformational syntax that this position is untenable. Restrictions among successive transformational applications
can be fully built into the structure indices of individual transformations only at the cost of otherwise unmotivated and enormously complicated additions to these transformations.
A second position is that the set of T-markers for each language must be determined by the existence of a special set
of grammatical rules for that language, these rules having
precisely the function of enumerating the sets of strings
which are the T-markers. To the extent that this position
is correct, a crucial question for the general theory of linguistic descriptions is the exact character of these rules.
At the moment, there are no published proposals concerning
this position, and it seems to us quite dubious. There is,
however, a third and much more interesting position on the
determination of T-markers. It is that the set of such T-
markers for each language is determined by general (i.e.,
universal) conditions in linguistic theory, these conditions
being stated in terms of different types of transformations,
deletions, permutations, embeddings, etc. This is the approach taken by Fillmore (1963). Although we do not feel
that his account is fully adequate, it is certainly in the right
direction. It is thus doubtful that individual languages contain any special rules for the enumeration of T-markers.

19.   The particular ordering established by (i) is of course ar-
      bitrary. We could as well have specified rightmost.

20.   The need for (ii) was not discussed when Diagram 3.18 and
      its derivatives were introduced, because at that point we
      had imposed the artificial restriction that each P-marker
      contain only one md.

21.   Katz and Fodor (1963), Katz (1964 b).

22.   By Chomsky and others.

Chapter 4

APPARENT COUNTEREXAMPLES

4.1 Introduction

In the previous chapter, we proposed a theory of how the projection rules of the semantic component operate. This theory was intended to provide the conceptual apparatus for expressing, within the theory of the semantic component, the generalization that transformations do not affect meaning. This generalization was accepted on the basis of a wide variety of cases which support it. There are, however, many apparent counterexamples in the literature. In this chapter we show that such cases are not genuine counterexamples but appear so only because their present formulation is not entirely adequate. We shall attempt to prove this by showing that the present conception of the semantic component implies a syntactic treatment of a representative sample of such cases that is preferable, even on purely syntactic grounds, to the formulation according to which they contradict our theory. We also show that certain revisions of the syntactic treatments of these cases yield not only a simpler and more powerful semantic component but also a simpler and explanatorily more powerful over-all linguistic description.

Counterexamples to a conception of the semantic component which claims that projection rules are restricted to underlying P-markers include syntactic treatments which provide underlying P-markers incapable of uniquely determining the correct semantic interpretations of these sentences in a general, formally motivated way. This will be the case if sentences with different meanings are assigned the same underlying P-markers, if sentences with the same meaning but without synonymous expressions have radically different underlying P-markers, if sentences with related meanings and grammatical form do not have parallel related underlying P-markers, and in general whenever the actual semantic properties of sentences cannot be described by the action of projection rules on the sequence of underlying P-markers. First we shall deal with cases involving exclusively singulary transformations. Then we shall turn to those involving generalized transformations.

4.2 Apparent Counterexamples in the Case of Singulary Transformations

4.2.1 Passive Cases.

The case of passives involving quantifiers and pronouns is rather often cited as an exception to the claim that singulary transformations do not affect the meaning of sentences. For example, Chomsky[1] claimed that a sentence like

(1) everyone in the room knows two languages

is not synonymous with its passive:

(2) two languages are known by everyone in the room

He argued that in (1) the languages known by different persons can both be different, while in (2) it is the same two languages for each person.

These examples are, however, unconvincing. Although the facts are far from clear, the active (1) seems to be open to the same interpretation attributed to the passive (2), and conversely, the passive is open to the same interpretation attributed to the active. Both (1) and (2) can mean either 'everyone in the room knows the same two particular languages, Persian and Hottentot' or 'everyone in the room knows two languages, different for different people'. Thus it seems that both actives and passives containing quantifiers and pronouns are ambiguous in the same way and so are full paraphrases of each other. If this is correct, there is no evidence based on quantifiers and pronouns that the passive transformation in any way alters the meaning of the underlying P-markers on which it operates, even if passives are derived by a transformation that applies to the underlying P-marker of the corresponding active.

But even if the meanings of examples like (1) and (2) are different, the argument that some transformations affect meaning does not hold. This argument must also assume that such examples are transformationally related, i.e., that the passives are derived from the application of a transformation to the P-marker underlying the corresponding active form. But strong syntactic motivation has been found which undercuts this assumption. A preferable treatment of passives (which we have, in fact, assumed in earlier examples) derives them, not from corresponding active forms, but rather from underlying P-markers containing an $Adverb_{manner}$ constituent dominating <u>by</u> plus a passive morpheme dummy.[2] But given such a treatment, the passive is not derived from a corresponding active form. Rather, it is derived from a P-marker with a passive morpheme dummy by a transformation whose structure index makes that transformation applicable only to P-markers with such a dummy. There-

fore, passives are not derived from actives, and the argument
that the transformation which produces passives will change the
meaning fails even if passives and their corresponding actives
are different in meaning.

However, though an active and its corresponding passive have
different underlying P-markers, the theory formulated in Chapter
3 commits us to two assumptions: First, if actives and their corresponding passives are the same in meaning, the differences between their underlying P-markers are semantically insignificant;
and second, if actives and their corresponding passives are different in meaning, the differences between their underlying P-
markers are semantically significant in the relevant respects.
Since we can find no difference in meaning between actives
and their corresponding passives, we must contend that the
Adverb$_{manner}$ constituent dominating by plus a passive dummy
and its syntactic relations to the syntactic structure of quantifiers and pronouns is without any semantic effect. The truth of
this contention is indicated by the fact that there is a generalization about the semantic properties of dummy morphemes, namely that the general theory of linguistic descriptions assigns each
such nonmatrix dummy a null reading, i.e., a reading which has
no semantic content but does not block the operation of P1. We
shall discuss this generalization and its justification in greater
detail later.

Stronger support for the position we are taking comes from a
consideration of the meaning of sentences which contain as an
embedded subpart strings which are essentially active structures
with quantifiers and pronouns. An example of such a case is

(3) there are two languages which everyone in the room knows

which is derived from

(4) there are two Rel languages

and (1) by an embedding transformation. The argument that in
the passive (2) the two languages referred to are the same two
for everyone, while in (1) the two languages are different for different individuals, and hence that (1) and (2) differ in meaning
is disconfirmed, because in (3) the languages referred to are
the same two for everybody and (3) could not have this interpretation if its constituent (1) did not have this meaning as well as
the other. This follows because it is clear from the character
of the semantic component that a particular constituent cannot
have a given reading in a sentence context unless that reading is
one of that constituent's readings in isolation.[3]

4.2.2 Negative Cases. The most interesting cases of singulary
transformations that must be considered in dicussing counterexamples to our theory of how the projection rules operate are those

of the question transformation, the imperative transformation, and the negative transformation — the major singulary transformations that relate pairs of sentences. In earlier treatments of these, one of the pair of related structures was always derived from the other transformationally. And in fact it was claimed that negatives, questions, and imperatives, as well as passives, were all derived from actives. But this implies that despite their differences in meaning from each other and from the active, all the corresponding members of these sentence types have the same underlying P-marker, namely that associated with the active. This is directly in conflict with the present view of semantic interpretation.

It is interesting that, quite independently of semantic considerations, certain more recent descriptions of English have found motivations for descriptions of some of these facts which are not incompatible with the view that projection rules operate exclusively on underlying P-markers. In particular, both Lees and Klima[4] have found it necessary to describe negative sentences by generating a negative morpheme in the phrase structure. But under this interpretation, the projection rules which operate on the readings for the negative morpheme need refer only to underlying P-markers.[5] The more recent treatment does not mean that there is no longer a negative transformation. There is. But instead of introducing a morpheme it now only repositions the morpheme, and instead of being optional it is now obligatory.

4.2.3 Imperative Cases. The question and the imperative thus present the chief remaining putative counterexamples among the transformations that relate major sentence types. In both cases, the recently published transformational descriptions present the imperative and question as rules to convert sentences of one type (with one meaning) into sentences of another type (with a different meaning). Unlike the Lees and Klima treatment of negation, the underlying P-markers operated on by question and imperative transformations in these formulations do not contain morphemes which can be assigned the meanings which differentiate actives, questions, and imperatives. These differences must thus be attributed to the effects of the transformations, and the semantic component must be thought of as either operating on derived P-markers or on the transformations themselves. Our theory of the way projection rules operate entails that this view of the question and imperative sentence types must be at least partly incorrect and that the rules for these phenomena should be formulated in a manner similar to that more recently provided for negative sentences. We claim that special question and imperative morphemes must occur in the underlying P-markers of question and imperative sentences respectively.

Consider first ordinary imperatives like

(5) go home

(6) you go home

(7) eat the meat

(8) you eat the meat

etc. It has been claimed that these imperatives are derived from the P-markers underlying such declarative sentences as, respectively,

(9) you will go home

(10) you will eat the meat

etc., by a transformation which deletes the Auxiliary constituent and optionally the subject Noun Phrase. The necessity of will in the underlying P-markers is shown by tag questions, where one finds

(11) go home, will you

but not

(12) *go home, did you

(13) *go home, must he

The necessity of a you subject is shown by the tag questions and most conclusively by reflexive forms, where one observes

(14) kill yourself

but not

(15) *kill herself

etc. The previously presented analysis of imperatives is thus, as far as it goes, both highly motivated and for the most part syntactically natural.

Besides the immediately evident semantic problems involved in the claim that all the various sentence types have the same underlying P-markers, there are some more subtle difficulties with imperatives. If (5) and (6) are derived from the same P-marker which underlies (9), and if there is no imperative morpheme in underlying P-markers which can bear the special meaning of imperative forms, then there is no non-ad hoc way to represent the fact that sentences like (9) are ambiguous and that the two terms of the ambiguity are differentiated precisely by the fact that one has an imperative and the other a declarative reading. This is a problem not only for a semantic component which restricts projection rules to underlying P-markers but for any semantic component, since it certainly cannot be maintained that any transformation has yielded the derived P-marker of (9) in

its imperative interpretation which has not also yielded the active interpretation. In short, if no imperative morpheme is
posited in underlying P-markers, there is no possible syntactic
basis for the ambiguity of sentences like (9) which will have unitary syntactic structures. Yet such sentences contain no lexical
items that can be considered ambiguous in the appropriate way.
It appears, therefore, that a linguistic description that recognizes
no imperative morpheme in underlying P-markers cannot in principle account for the ambiguity of sentences of the form you will
Main Verb.

To account for the relevant facts and bring the syntactic treatment of imperatives in line with our conception of the semantic
component, we posit an imperative morpheme, I, in all, and
only, underlying P-markers of imperative sentences. Thus sentences like (9) have two different underlying P-markers, one with
and one without I.

We can assign I a dictionary entry that represents it as having
roughly the sense of 'the speaker requests (asks, demands, insists, etc.) that'.[6] We shall abbreviate this reading as RIM.
This reading has the desirable consequence of making it possible
to account conveniently for the paraphrase relations between such
sentences as

(16) I request you go home

(17) you go home

(18) go home

The device of providing I with a reading like RIM also makes
it possible to account for certain anomalies in imperative sentences:

(19) *believe the claim

(20) *understand the answer

(21) *want more money

(22) *hope it rains

Examples (19)-(22) are clearly anomalous in just the same way
and for just the same reason as are

(23) *I request that you believe the claim

(24) *I request that you understand the answer

(25) *I request that you want more money

(26) *I request that you hope it rains

But such sentences as

(27) learn the sum

(28) know your lesson

(29) imagine the situation

(30) forget the whole matter

are definitely not anomalous, just as their counterparts are not:

(31) I request that you learn the sum

(32) I request that you know your lesson

(33) I request that you imagine the situation

(34) I request that you forget the whole matter

The anomaly of (23)-(26) is due to the fact that part of the meaning of <u>request</u> makes it anomalous to request someone to do something which he cannot willfully choose to do. Being in such psychological states as belief, understanding, wanting, and hoping is not subject to a person's will. These facts can easily be represented in terms of semantic relations between the readings of verbs like <u>request</u> and the readings for their complement <u>that-</u> clauses which will be marked as to whether or not they describe psychological states of the appropriate kind. But, unless <u>I</u> is assigned the reading RIM, there is no basis for marking such anomalies when they appear in the imperative paraphrases (19)-(22) of the request sentences.

The point to be stressed, however, is that besides the many semantic justifications for postulating the occurrence of <u>I</u> in underlying P-markers, this postulation can be justified in exclusively syntactic terms. First, there are no imperatives with various kinds of sentence adverbials although these occur readily with <u>you will</u> ... declarative forms:

(35) $\left\{ \begin{array}{l} \text{maybe} \\ \text{yes} \\ \text{perhaps} \\ \text{certainly} \end{array} \right\}$ you will drive the car

(36) no you will not drive the car

but

(37) * $\left\{ \begin{array}{l} \text{maybe} \\ \text{yes} \\ \text{perhaps} \\ \text{certainly} \end{array} \right\}$ drive the car

(38) *no do not drive the car[7]

Second, there are certain <u>negative preverbs</u>[8] with which imperatives do not co-occur, although declaratives do:

(39) you will $\left\{ \begin{array}{l} \text{hardly} \\ \text{scarcely} \end{array} \right\}$ touch your food

but

(40) $*\begin{Bmatrix} \text{hardly} \\ \text{scarcely} \end{Bmatrix}$ touch your food

Third, there are certain verbs, especially a certain subclass
of those with complements, that have no imperatives, although
they have corresponding active <u>you will . . .</u> forms:

(41) * want to go

(42) * hope to be famous

but

(43) you will want to go

(44) you will hope to be famous

Unlike (9) above, (43) and (44) are not ambiguous and have no
imperative interpretation.[9] There are, no doubt, other similar
selectional restrictions that differentiate declarative from imperative forms. Postulation of an imperative morpheme permits these selections to be stated in the phrase structure in terms
of co-occurrence restrictions on $\underline{I}$ and sentence adverbials, preverbs, subclasses of verbs, etc. The presence of $\underline{I}$ will presumably also simplify description of the fact that imperatives
do not occur as the constituent elements for embedding transformations except in the special (but, no doubt, universal) case
of quotational contexts like

(45) he said: drink the beer

The imperative morpheme will also help in stating sentence-
type restrictions under co-ordination, i.e., the fact that one
finds

(46) put on your coat and go out

(47) the boy put on his coat and went out

(48) come here and I'll give you a dollar

but not

(49) * I'll give you a dollar and come here

The restriction appears to be that the imperative can only be the
second term of such co-ordinations if the first member is also
an imperative.

Thus there seems to be a good syntactic justification for a
treatment of imperatives in which phrase structure rules generate an imperative morpheme at the beginning of certain sentence
structures. The imperative transformation, which applies oblig-
atorily to any P-marker containing the imperative morpheme,

drops this morpheme and, optionally, drops the string you Present will or just the string Present will.

4.2.4 Question Cases. The treatment of questions in the literature on generative grammar[10] derives them by the application of singulary transformations on P-markers that underlie the corresponding declaratives. Thus questions pose apparent counterexamples to our contention that P1 operate exclusively on underlying P-markers because, in this current treatment, a question and its corresponding declarative have the same sequence of underlying P-marker(s), and yet it is obvious that a question and its corresponding declarative differ in meaning.

To show that questions do not constitute true counterexamples to our contention, we must formulate an alternative treatment of questions and justify it against the previous one. Such an alternative treatment immediately suggests itself if we recall that cases of imperative and negative sentences appeared to be counterexamples for the same reasons that questions now appear to be. In other words, such sentences seemed to have the same sequence of underlying P-markers as their corresponding declaratives, and yet they clearly did not have the same meaning. In the cases of imperatives and negatives, a newer syntactic treatment derived the former from structures containing an imperative morpheme and the latter from those containing a negative morpheme. In this way, it was shown that these cases are not genuine counterexamples since the sequence of underlying P-markers for imperative sentences is different from that for their corresponding declaratives and since the same is true for negative sentences. If we uniformly extend this mode of treatment, we can likewise prove that questions are not genuine counterexamples by showing that they are derived from structures containing a morpheme analogous to I and Negative, called Q, and therefore that questions and their corresponding declaratives do not have the same sequence of underlying P-markers. We shall develop such a treatment later.

Before considering such a treatment of questions, it is necessary to discuss an important principle governing the operation of deletion and substitution transformations. This principle requires that the distortions produced by the transformational removal of elements from a P-marker be unique. That is, a transformation T which operates by deleting elements or substituting for elements can apply to a P-marker only if the output of T on that P-marker permits unique recovery of that P-marker, given a description of T. The motivation for this principle requiring unique recoverability, which receives its formulation in the general theory of linguistic descriptions, is both syntactic and semantic. The syntactic motivation comes primarily from evidence about particular natural languages which shows that the simplest grammars of the transformational type for these languages conform to the requirement of this principle.[11] Of course, there is not yet enough evidence of this kind to settle the issue decisively. But the best hypothesis at this stage is clearly the one which says that deletion and substitution rules of any syntactic component must permit unique recoverability. This is the best hypothesis because it is the narrowest constraint on the form of syntactic components consistent with the available evidence, and thus it is the strongest claim about the nature of human language. An indication of the strength of the claim made by imposing the requirement of unique recoverability on every syntactic component is that this requirement renders the set of sentences generated by a syntactic component recursive. This claim about human language is of much formal significance since it has this consequence. The semantic motivation for this principle will be discussed later.

Unique recoverability is not possible if transformations can delete or substitute for any arbitrary elements in a P-marker. We propose to guarantee unique recoverability by introducing a universal constituent, for which we use the term 'Pro', and by imposing a constraint on transformational derivations in which deletion or substitution operations occur.

Chomsky[12] has written the following:

> "... major categories have associated with them a 'dummy terminal symbol' as a member (which may actually be realized, e.g. 'it' for abstract nouns, 'someone' ('thing') and ... this representative of the category is what actually must appear in the underlying strings for those transformations where the transform carries no indication of the actual terminal representative of this category in the underlying string."

By 'major category' Chomsky means a lexical category — i.e., Noun, Verb, Adjective, etc. — or any category that dominates a lexical category. The function of the constituent Pro is to characterize formally at the syntactic level the class of all, and only, such representatives of major categories. This universal syntactic characterization of 'pro-forms' is necessary because, aside from the semantic features of these forms, such forms have universal syntactic properties. Chief among these universal syntactic properties is that only such pro-forms are 'freely deletable'.[13] Actually, free deletability of pro-forms appears to be restricted to the nominal system, but it is not yet known how this restriction on free deletability is to be formalized in the syntactic component. A prerequisite for such a formalization is a universal characterization of such notions as 'Noun Phrase', 'Noun', 'Verb', which we shall discuss later.

The constraint on transformational derivations is as follows:

A transformation T whose elementary transformations include a deletion or substitution affecting the ith term of T's structure index applies to a P-marker PM bracketed in terms of the structure index of T just in case one of the following conditions is met:

(i) The ith term of the structure index of T is a string of terminal symbols.

(ii) The string of terminal symbols of the ith term of the bracketing of PM is necessarily identical with a different string of terminal symbols also occurring in PM. [14]

(iii) The string of terminal symbols of the ith term of the bracketing of PM is dominated by Pro.

In other words, a transformation can delete or substitute something for a non-pro-form John only if the structure index of the transformation itself mentions John (as the imperative transformation's structure index actually mentions the morphemes you and will) or if John is necessarily repeated at some other point in the P-marker from which it is being removed, as in the underlying P-marker of

(50) John cut himself

which is schematically John Past cut John. This kind of restriction is semantically necessary to account for the fact that sentences like

(51) John is reading

derived from the structure John is reading Noun Phrase, are not indefinitely ambiguous. That is, (51) does not mean 'John is reading books or magazines or a tombstone, etc.' Hence, it cannot be the case that any of these morpheme sequences were actually deleted in the derivation of (51), and similarly in analogous cases. Instead, (51) must be derived by deleting one of the pro-forms of a Noun Phrase, in this case either something or it. By 'free deletability' we mean the kind of deletion that is not in accord with Condition (i) or (ii).

Pro-forms require special attention here because their contribution to the semantic interpretation of the underlying P-markers in which they occur is somewhat different from that of ordinary lexical items. We must determine what kinds of semantic information the occurrences of pro-forms contribute and how to construct the formal machinery of the semantic component so that such information can be associated with occurrences of pro-forms in such a way that it can be utilized in the process of semantic interpretation.

Consider these sentences:

(52) the man is reading something

(53) the man is listening to something

(54) he did it

The underlying P-markers for (52) and (53) are as shown in Diagrams 4.1 and 4.2, respectively.[15] Someone who hears (52), or

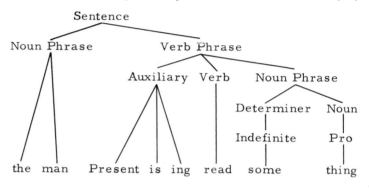

Diagram 4.1

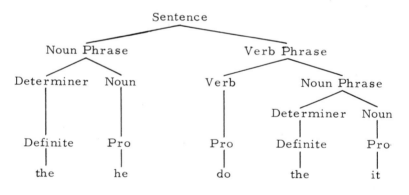

Diagram 4.2

its paraphrase on a reading (51), learns that what is being read is something with writing on it; one who hears (53) learns that what is being listened to is an audible sound; but someone who hears (54) learns only that some male being performs a specific act.[16] There is a definite regularity which represents the meaning of each occurrence of a pro-form in (51)-(54) regardless of whether the pro-form is finally deleted. The semantic information that someone obtains in the case of a pro-form is just the combination of semantic information which comes from the reading of the particular pro-form, i. e. , the semantic markers as-

signed to the pro-form in its dictionary entry, plus those semantic markers which state the selection restriction on amalgamation with the set of readings for the element in the position to be
amalgamated with that pro-form.

To express the above regularity we stipulate in the general
theory of linguistic descriptions that the dictionary entry of every
pro-form (i. e., every form dominated by the constituent Pro)
must contain the semantic marker (Selector) which is defined
by this equivalence:

$$\text{Lexical string} \rightarrow \text{Syntactic markers} \rightarrow (m_1) \rightarrow \dots \rightarrow (\text{Selector})$$
$$\rightarrow \dots \rightarrow (m_k) \rightarrow [1]\langle\Omega\rangle \equiv \text{Lexical string} \rightarrow \text{Syntactic mark-}$$
$$\text{kers} \rightarrow (m_1) \rightarrow \dots \rightarrow (\Omega) \rightarrow \dots \rightarrow (m_k) \rightarrow [1]\langle\Omega\rangle.$$

Once the reading of a pro-form is amalgamated into the reading
of some other constituent, or vice versa, the derived reading
having the form of the first term of the equivalance defining (Selector) must be replaced by another reading having the form of
the second term of the stated equivalence. This amalgamation
of the readings of pro-forms is performed by whichever P1 is
relevant in terms of the syntactic structure of the P-marker
containing them. No special projection rules are needed just
to handle the semantic interpretation of underlying P-markers
containing occurrences of pro-forms.

Consider again Example (52). The semantic interpretation
of the underlying P-marker of this sentence, and its paraphrase
(51), must represent the fact that what is being read is a physical object with writing on it, but not that it is specifically a book,
tombstone, tomato juice can label, etc. This is accomplished
in the following way. The readings for some and thing in the
object Noun Phrase are combined by the P1 which amalgamates
readings for the Determiner and Noun to produce a derived reading containing (Selector) which is assigned to the dominating node
labeled 'Noun Phrase'. Then the P1 which combines the readings of a Verb with those of its object Noun Phrase combines
this derived reading with a reading assigned to the lexical item
read. For the most common sense of read, its reading has the
selection restriction requiring its object Noun Phrase to have
a reading containing semantic markers that represent physical
objects with writing on them. By the equivalence which defines
(Selector), the reading which results from the Verb plus Noun
Phrase amalgamation is converted into another reading identical
to the first except that the occurrence of (Selector) is replaced
by the markers representing the selection restriction in the reading which represents the aforementioned sense of read.[17] This
reading is then combined with the reading of the subject Noun
Phrase (we ignore here the Auxiliary for simplicity) in the usual
fashion, producing a Sentence reading which has exactly the prop-

erties that, as we have seen, are empirically required. Thus
it is clear that the semantic interpretation of (52) and (51) (since
this has the same underlying P-marker) does represent the fact
that what is being read is a physical object with writing on it and
does not specify the character of this object further. Similarly,
(53) is provided with an interpretation ensuring that what is being
listened to is an audible sound, since the selection restriction of
the lexical item listen to requires an object Noun Phrase whose
reading contains semantic markers representing audible sounds,
but nothing further. The equivalence defining (Selector) is thus
the mechanism which specifies the semantic contribution of an
occurrence of a pro-form in an underlying P-marker. This contribution is the compound marker formed from the selection condition of the reading of the element in the position to be amalgamated with the reading of the occurrence of the pro-form, plus
the semantic markers assigned to the pro-form by its dictionary
entry.[18]

We observe at this point that the semantic marker (Selector)
and the semantic mechanisms associated with it, together with
the syntactic mechanisms concerning the element Pro and its
relations to free deletability, provide a promising beginning for
a universal characterization of the notion 'pro-form'. Such a
characterization not only would specify the membership of the
category of 'pro-forms' but would systematize the relations between this category and other features of the semantic and syntactic components. But much obviously remains to be done to
complete and justify this characterization.

Previously, the description of questions in generative terms
has involved a basic division into two types, yes-no questions
like

(55) did Bill see John

(56) will Bill see John

etc., and wh-questions including

(57) who saw John

(58) who did John see

(59) when did John see Bill

(60) where did John see Bill

(61) why did John see Bill

(62) how did John see Bill

(63) what did John see Bill with

(64) which man did John see

(65) what kind of binoculars did John see Bill with

(66) whose binoculars did John see Bill with

etc. We shall see that, although there is a basis for distinguish-
ing yes-no questions from wh-questions, it is not exactly that
which has been previously assumed.

It will be convenient, however, first to discuss questions in
terms of this previously established division. The problem which
yes-no questions raise for our theory of semantic interpretation,
given their past description, is easily seen by comparing (55)
and (56) with the declaratives:

(67) Bill saw John

(68) Bill will see John

Under the past syntactic treatment, Examples (55) and (67) and
Examples (56) and (68) have, respectively, the same underlying
P-markers, although they obviously differ in meaning.

Let us examine this contrast in meaning more closely. An
important fact about questions is that, semantically, they are
somewhat like imperatives in that questions are requests of a
special kind. However, unlike imperatives, which, in general,
request some form of nonlinguistic behavior or action, questions
are concerned primarily with linguistic responses.[19] Thus while
the imperative

(69) go home

has as a paraphrase something like

(70) I request that you go home

the question

(71) will you go home

has as a paraphrase something like

(72) I request that you answer 'X I will go home'

where X is one of special class of sentence adverbials including
yes, no, of course, etc. We claim that not just any sentence
adverbial is appropriate as an instance of X, since the indefinite
elements maybe, perhaps, possibly, etc., are, when used as
answers, in effect evasions and do not represent the kind of re-
sponse the speaker requested. In fact, even elements like of
course represent a strict deviation from the kind of answer requested in that they provide information the speaker didn't ask
for. That is, not only is the answer positive but the asker should
have known it. There is thus good reason to claim that X in (72)
takes as values only yes or no so that it is an exact paraphrase
of

(73) I request that you answer 'yes I will go home' or 'no I
      will not go home' [20]

Clearly, the semantic description of yes-no questions like (71)
and the marking of paraphrase relations such as those illustrated
by (73) will be most adequately accomplished if there is a morpheme Q in the underlying P-markers of yes-no questions which
can be given a reading appropriate to distinguish yes-no questions
from their corresponding declaratives and to represent the paraphrase relations with I request ... sentences.

We now turn to the consideration of the other major class of
questions, wh-questions like (57)-(66). The problem raised by
these questions is evident from their past treatment in transformational descriptions, which has been to postulate the introduction by transformation of a single wh morpheme into P-markers
to which various elements may be attached.[21]   This attachment
then indicates that the element attached 'is being questioned'.

However, a treatment of wh-questions in terms of one wh, transformationally added or not, is incompatible with the assertion that
the ordered set of underlying P-markers alone determines semantic interpretation. For example, this description provides no distinction in underlying P-markers between sentences like

(74) who saw someone

(75) who did someone see

which would both presumably have at best an underlying P-marker like that shown in Diagram 4.3. And in general in previous

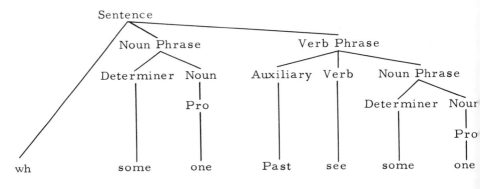

Diagram 4.3

transformational treatments there is no unique indication in the
underlying P-marker as to which element is 'questioned'. Thus
the older treatment does not indicate in the underlying P-markers that in (74) the subject Noun Phrase is 'questioned', while
in (75) the object Noun Phrase is. These naturally require, how-

ever, very different semantic interpretations, for the former is rightfully a paraphrase of

(76) I request that you answer 'X saw someone'

while the latter is a paraphrase of

(77) I request that you answer 'someone saw X'

where in each case X is an appropriate exponent of Noun Phrase.

The theory that semantic interpretations are determined by the operation of projection rules exclusively on the sequence of underlying P-markers requires that those elements which are 'questioned' be specified in underlying P-markers. Thus (74) and (75) cannot have the same underlying P-marker, and the difference between them must provide a non-ad hoc treatment of the fact that one is a paraphrase of (76), the other of (77). Furthermore, the facts about paraphrase mentioned earlier clearly suggest that wh-questions must, on semantic grounds, contain the same element Q as yes-no questions in order to represent the reading of 'request an answer'. Yet wh-questions and simple truth-value questions cannot have the same underlying P-markers either. Therefore, although Q is necessary to characterize similarities between all questions, it is certainly not sufficient to distinguish among them properly. Thus neither

(78) did someone see someone

nor

(79) who saw whom

is a paraphrase of either (74) or (75) or each other. Moreover, the presence of Q in the underlying P-markers of all four cannot account for these facts about paraphrase relations. Other differentiae must be found.

We have discussed some requirements which semantic adequacy places on the description of questions. Let us now consider purely syntactic arguments for a treatment of questions compatible with the requirement that semantic interpretations be determined uniquely by the operation of projection rules on the sequence of underlying P-markers. Consider again simple truth-value questions. The syntactic arguments for postulating Q in the underlying P-markers of these questions are similar to those for postulating I in the underlying P-markers of imperatives. Sentence adverbials also do not occur in ordinary yes-no questions (although some do in tag questions, with which we do not deal in detail):

(80) a. $\left\{ \begin{array}{l} \text{certainly} \\ \text{probably} \\ \text{yes} \\ \text{maybe} \end{array} \right\}$ he is a doctor

   b. no he is not a doctor

   c. *$\left\{\begin{array}{l}\text{certainly}\\\text{probably}\\\text{yes}\\\text{maybe}\end{array}\right\}$ is he a doctor

   d. *no is he not a doctor

   e. John is $\left\{\begin{array}{l}\text{certainly}\\\text{probably}\end{array}\right\}$ a doctor, isn't he

We do not deal with tag questions here, but it is possible that
they are optional variants of some ordinary yes-no questions.
The difference in freedom with sentence adverbials can then perhaps be accounted for by making the rule of tag formation obligatory in the presence of sentence adverbials of the type certainly. Similarly, there are negative preverbs and other elements which declaratives, but not questions, may contain:

   (81) a. he $\left\{\begin{array}{l}\text{scarcely}\\\text{hardly}\end{array}\right\}$ eats

         b. *does he $\left\{\begin{array}{l}\text{scarcely}\\\text{hardly}\end{array}\right\}$ eat

         c. he sometimes eats

         d. *does he sometimes eat

and also elements of the opposite type:

   (82) a. *he ever eats

         b. does he ever eat

         c. *he eats $\left\{\begin{array}{l}\text{any meat}\\\text{anywhere}\end{array}\right\}$

         d. does he eat $\left\{\begin{array}{l}\text{any meat}\\\text{anywhere}\end{array}\right\}$ [22]

   These selectional facts can evidently best be stated if there
is a Q morpheme in the underlying P-markers of simple truth-
value questions. The presence of Q can likewise simplify the
statement that questions are not embedded except in quotational
contexts:

   (83) a. he asked 'can I go to the movies now'

         b. *I saw the picture which can the man paint

Similarly, Q will simplify the statement of the restrictions on
combinations of elements like

   (84) a. if he comes will you come

     b. if he comes you will come

     c. *if does he come will you come

     d. *if does he come you will come

The syntactic arguments suggesting that Q should occur in the underlying P-markers of simple truth-value questions also show that it must occur in the underlying P-markers of wh-questions:

(85) *$\left\{ \begin{array}{l} \text{certainly} \\ \text{probably} \\ \text{yes} \\ \text{maybe} \end{array} \right\}$ $\left\{ \begin{array}{l} \text{who is a doctor} \\ \text{where is the doctor} \end{array} \right\}$

(86) * what does John $\left\{ \begin{array}{l} \text{scarcely} \\ \text{hardly} \end{array} \right\}$ eat[23]

etc.

The fact that Q must occur in the underlying P-markers of both wh-questions and ordinary truth-value questions raises the issue of how these are to be distinguished from each other. This is the syntactic parallel of the question about their semantic differentiation raised but not answered earlier. The problems, both syntactic and semantic, are by no means solved even when wh-questions are distinguished from ordinary truth-value questions by positing a further morpheme, wh, in the former. For while this device permits the differentiation of (74), (75), and (79) from (78), it does not specify how (74), (75), and (79) are to be distinguished from each other. In terms of the present theory of linguistic descriptions, their underlying P-markers must contain either partially different sets of morphemes or else sets of morphemes partially different in order. The latter is, of course, the natural suggestion. We therefore claim that the difference between (74), (75), and (79), or, more generally, the difference between different types of wh-questions, is exactly the difference between the position and number of occurrences of wh in underlying P-markers. The underlying P-markers of wh-questions contain both the morpheme Q and the morpheme wh. The Q morpheme indicates semantically only that the sentence is a question, i.e., a paraphrase of an appropriate sentence of the form I request that you answer ... . The function of wh is, however, to specify the element or elements of the sentence that are 'questioned'.

Thus for any underlying P-marker schematically of the form

(87)   X
               /\
   Q ... wh ... ...

where wh is specially associated with the constituent X, the sentence represented by this underlying P-marker must be a paraphrase of

(88) I request that you give an answer,, i.e., produce a true
      sentence one of whose readings is identical with the read-
      ing of (87) except that the content of Q is not present and
      the reading associated with X in (87) is supplemented by
      further semantic material, i.e., semantic markers.

In short, if one is asked

(89) who killed Lincoln

i.e.,
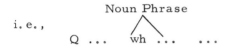

one replies

(90) Booth killed Lincoln

and if asked

(91) when did Booth kill Lincoln

i.e.,
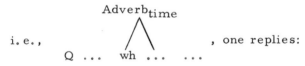
, one replies:

(92) Booth killed Lincoln in 1865

In each case the answer must be semantically related to the question by deleting the markers representing 'request an answer'
and by adding further markers to the reading of the constituent
X, which dominates an occurrence of wh in the question. Hence,
the answer to (89) adds to the semantic markers of the questioned
subject Noun Phrase, namely (Human), (Animate), etc., the markers (Named 'Booth'), etc. We discuss the semantic relations between question and answer in greater detail later, providing a
much more precise account of these relations in terms of readings for Q, functioning of wh, and a projection rule for the amalgamation of the reading of Q.

There is, of course, a habit of answering questions according
to which the full forms like (90) and (92) are not used. Instead
one uses the respective short forms

(93) Booth

(94) in 1865

which should not be thought of as fully grammatical, i.e., as
sentences. Rather, they must be regarded as contextually reduced versions of (90) and (92), i.e., as semisentences.[24] In
these reduced forms only the content of the category which wh

marked as being 'questioned' in the question form is actually present in the answer.[25]

The conception of the syntactic treatment of wh-questions involved in the preceding discussion raises a number of fundamental syntactic problems. In the older way of treating wh-questions, a single wh was introduced at the beginning of a sentence, and the category to be 'questioned' was attached to this. The treatment we have suggested implies that wh 'is associated with' the particular elements it specifies semantically in underlying P-markers. Thus its varying 'associations' must be accounted for in terms of varying positions in underlying P-markers. In terms of the conception of the syntactic component accepted in this study, apparently an occurrence of wh must appear on the right side of rules which introduce various constituents in the constituent structure subcomponent of the syntax. Although this new treatment of wh appears more complicated than the older, we shall nevertheless see various reasons why it is not really complicated at all. Furthermore, the older treatment can hardly be considered simpler than the newer, because it actually does not describe the full range of facts. It provides no way of handling the fact that there can be more than one occurrence of wh in a single underlying P-marker:

(95) who did what to whom

(96) where did who do what

Since we see no reason not to accept (95), (96), and all analogous forms as bona fide English, it is evident that no description which introduces a single occurrence of wh at the beginning of sentences can be considered descriptively adequate. Sentences like (95) and (96) show that there is independent syntactic motivation for introducing more than one occurrence of wh in a single underlying P-marker and for associating each occurrence with a different constituent of that underlying P-marker.

Although a detailed treatment of wh-questions is not possible here, some of their important features must be discussed. We suggest that wh-questions contain two classes distinguished by the difference between definite (the) and indefinite (a/some) articles. The single-word question forms who, what, where, when, why, how, etc., fall into the indefinite group. We can illustrate this contrast best with the display of forms in Diagram 4.4.

There are several major facts revealed by this display. There is a general contrast between two possible kinds of questions which seems to correlate with the definite-indefinite article contrast. Furthermore, the indefinite article a/some (a and some are the alternative forms) is attached to a following pro-form, that is a noun occurrence dominated by the constituent Pro. This accounts for the fact that someone is a single word, some book

	Noun Phrase	
	Article	Noun
1. a. which book b. what book c. a book	"	book
2. a. which one b. *what one →what c. something	"	Pro | one/thing/it
3. a. which man b. what man c. a man	"	man
4. a. which one b. *what one →who c. some {one / body}	a. wh + the b. wh + a/some c.　　 a/some	Pro | one/body
5. a. which place b. *what place →where c. some {place / where}	"	Pro | place/where/there
6. a. which place b. what place c. some place	"	place
7. a. which time b. *what time →when c. sometime	"	Pro | time/when/then
8. a. which time b. what time c. some time	"	time
9. a. which way b. *what way →how c. somehow	"	Pro | way/how
10. a. which way b. what way c. some way	"	way
11. a. which reason b. *what reason → why c. *some {why / reason}	"	Pro | reason/why
12. a. which reason b. what reason c. some reason	"	reason
13. a. which one's book b. *what one's book →whose book c. some {one / body} 's book	"	Pro | one/body

Diagram 4.4

two words. But if the single-word wh-question forms are derived from indefinite articles with a preceding attached <u>wh</u>, the fact that they <u>are</u> single words follows automatically from the rule which must be in the grammar anyway to yield the nonquestion indefinite pro-forms <u>someone</u>, <u>something</u>, <u>somehow</u>, etc. Furthermore, the single-word question forms in a number of cases fill a gap left by the absence of an actual <u>what</u> + pro-form sequence. Hence, the absence of * <u>what one</u> (Human) is filled by <u>who</u>, and the absence of * <u>what one's</u> is filled by <u>whose</u>, etc. The situation is complicated, however, by the fact that some of the relevant pro-forms have, or so we claim, nearly identical nouns which are not pro-forms. In this way we can account for the presence of <u>some thing</u> alongside <u>something</u>, <u>some place</u> alongside <u>some(place/ where)</u>, etc. Some further evidence for the association of the single-word question forms with noun phrases containing indefinite articles and pro-forms follows from the distribution of <u>else</u> (which is evidently a reduced and repositioned form of <u>other</u>):

(97) a. someone else saw Harry
      b. Harry saw him someplace else
      c. * the man else saw Harry
      d. * he else saw Harry
      e. * Harry saw him at the place else
      f. who else saw Harry
      g. where else did Harry see him

etc.[26]

It should be emphasized that deriving the single-word question forms from pro-elements is, in effect, required by the constraint on deletions and substitutions already discussed. In some past descriptions it has been assumed that <u>who</u>, <u>what</u>, etc., were derived from arbitrary instances of Noun Phrase. But this would violate the constraint that transformational operations be reconstructible, since with such question forms there is no way to determine by inspecting the grammar which particular instance of Noun Phrase underlies any particular question form. In our terms, the derivation from arbitrary instances of Noun Phrase would have the false implication that each instance of such question forms is infinitely ambiguous, whereas in fact they simply seem to be unspecific. It is interesting, therefore, that the general constraint on transformational distortions excludes this older analysis which yields false semantic predictions and which fails to bring out the fact that the relevant question forms fill certain gaps in the distribution of pro-forms (as shown in Diagram 4.4), as well as other important syntactic facts discussed above and in the references listed in footnote 26. The syntactic evidence of gaps, <u>else</u>, etc., which supports the derivation of single-word question forms from indefinite article + pro-form, thus also supports the principle of reconstructible transformational operations.

The association of the contrast in wh-questions with the definite-indefinite article contrast appears to correlate correctly
with the semantic contrast between definite and indefinite article.
That is, the difference between the contrasting pairs in

(98) a. who did you see
      b. which one did you see
      c. whose book did you steal
      d. which one's book did you steal
      e. where did you see him
      f. which place did you see him at

appears to be precisely that between 'questioning' a definitely
marked domain versus 'questioning' an indefinitely marked domain. And the fact that the single-word question forms fit semantically into the indefinite class supports the syntactic evidence suggesting their relation to indefinite articles.

If the preceding analysis can be maintained, the majority of
wh-questions — in fact, almost all those other than the type based
on non-manner adverbial how (how big, how often, etc.) — can
be accounted for directly in terms of the association of wh with
the Determiner constituent. Regardless of how other questions
must be described, this permits a very elegant generalization
about the range of constituents which can be 'questioned' and apparently eliminates the need for permitting the 'questioning' of
a wide variety of distinct adverbial constituents besides the Noun
Phrase constituent. Thus there is support for the previous contention that associating wh with constituents in underlying P-
markers does not complicate the description.

In our preliminary account of the meaning of questions in (88)
we spoke of a constituent X to which wh was attached. In most
wh-questions the wh morpheme appears to be attached to the
Determiner constituent, which dominates at least articles, demonstratives, and the Rel constituent. The implication of (88)
is that when wh is attached to X in the presence of Q (this being
interpreted to mean that X is the lowest node that dominates wh),
wh serves to indicate that X is 'questioned'. We claimed that a
reading assigned to the constituent in the answer to a question
which corresponds to the constituent X in the question itself must
differ from the reading assigned to X only by the addition of some
semantic markers. It could be argued, however, that when the
wh of a question is attached to an article preceding a pro-form,
the answer might further specify not only the Determiner but
also the pro-form. It might also be argued that in some cases
an answer may 'underspecify' the element following a 'questioned'
determiner by replacing a non-pro-form with a corresponding pro-
form. Hence, it might be claimed that in

(99) a. which man saw John
      b. which one saw John

      c.   the man who I saw yesterday saw John
      d.   the one who I saw yesterday saw John

both c and d are appropriate answers to a and b. Thus one might conclude that a full account of the semantic properties of questions must amend (88) to allow for the addition of further semantic markers to the pro-form following a 'questioned' Determiner, and perhaps for the deletion of markers from a non-pro-form following such a 'questioned' element.

    Neither of these objections is valid, however. Both rest on a failure to distinguish between information supplied by a context (which in this case has been tacitly assumed), on the one hand, and information supplied by the linguistic structure of sentences, on the other. In Example (99), one thinks of d as an answer to a, and c as an answer to b, because one tacitly assumes a context in which the referents of the pro-forms in c and d (i.e., the things that are referred to by these pro-forms in the assumed context) are fixed and have the interpretation in which one equals 'man'. But it is easy to see that b and d could occur in a context in which one might, for example, have an animal or woman as its referent. Thus, without any assumption about context, d cannot be conceived of as an answer to a, and c cannot be conceived of as an answer to b. In terms of the linguistic structure of the sentences in (99), only c is an answer to a, and only d is an answer to b. Therefore, the above objections against our treatment of the meaning of questions can receive no empirical support from cases such as those in (99).

    One of the most striking implications of this suggested treatment of wh-questions is that it shows that so-called yes-no or simple truth-value questions are also wh-questions. They are naturally regarded as wh-questions in which the constituent 'questioned' is the Sentence Adverbial, a constituent whose exponents have readings containing semantic markers that pertain to truth value, degree of certainty, etc. Such a treatment has the correct consequence that the answers to yes-no questions are in fact sentence adverbials, i.e., yes, no, and perhaps by extension maybe, of course, certainly, etc. (but see our earlier comment about these forms as yes-no question answers).

    In support of the claim that yes-no questions are wh-questions, observe that all the wh-question types appear in nominalizations in almost their question form (the permutation of the Auxiliary with the subject and the subsequent introduction of do in certain cases do not occur here):

(100)

$$\text{I noticed} \left\{ \begin{array}{l} \left\{ \begin{array}{l} \text{where} \\ \text{when} \\ \text{how} \\ \text{why} \end{array} \right\} \text{he went} \\ \text{who went} \\ \text{whether he went} \end{array} \right\}$$

But the last form in (100) must be considered to be dominated by
Sentence Adverbial, one of whose elements is <u>either-or</u>. This is
shown clearly by such sets as

    (101) a. either John came or not
           b. I noticed whether John came or not

Such considerations suggest rather clearly that <u>whether</u> in occurrences like (100) and (101)b must have an underlying structure something like that shown in Diagram 4.5. Not enough is

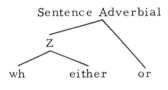

yet known about the internal structure
of the Sentence Adverbial constituent
to specify Z in detail (or even to justify
its occurrence) and hence to give a more
adequate version of Diagram 4.5.

Diagram 4.5

      As mentioned earlier, simple yes-no
questions cannot contain actual exponents of Sentence Adverbial, in particu-
lar <u>yes</u> and <u>no</u>. Notice also that <u>either-or</u>, <u>yes</u>, and <u>no</u> are all
mutually exclusive in declarative sentences. Treating <u>either-
or</u>, <u>yes</u>, and <u>no</u> as sentence adverbials and deriving ordinary
yes-no questions from <u>either-or</u> accounts automatically for all
these facts, and this in turn provides further support for the
claim that simple yes-no questions are based on underlying P-
markers containing a Sentence Adverbial constituent dominating
<u>wh</u>. Additional support for this claim will be provided in our
discussion of the syntactic rules for questions later in this section.

    Incidentally, there are certain types of questions that we shall
not handle here. Earlier we suggested that tag questions might
be optional variants of simple yes-no questions. However, the
situation is quite complicated and inherently involves so-called
negative questions as well as emphasis. Consider the contrasts
in

    (102) a. did she sleep (or not)
           b. didn't she sleep
           c. she <u>did</u> sleep, didn't she
           d. <u>did</u> she sleep
           e. she didn't sleep, did she
           f. she slept, didn't she

The underlining in these examples is to indicate contrastive or
emphatic stress. It certainly does not seem correct to view all
of them as paraphrases. While some of the differences are ob-
scure, we can make several fairly clear observations. The two
sentences represented by (102)a are in a sense 'neutral' with
respect to what is 'questioned'. The rest of these questions
seem, however, to involve certain 'presumptions'. In (102)b,

c, and f the presumptions appear to be as follows. Something in the context has indicated that the activity being 'questioned' did not occur, while the questioner up till then had reason to believe it did. In (102)d and e, the situation is reversed. Here something indicates that the 'questioned' activity did occur, while the questioner up till then had reason to believe it did not. Thus the tag, negative, and emphatic questions appear to be semantically related in that they indicate not simply that the questioner wants certain information, as do simple yes-no questions like (102)a, but also a state of belief on the part of the questioner which is in conflict with certain other information about the topic of the question. Furthermore, these types of questions indicate whether the questioner's state of belief was originally either positively or negatively oriented toward the topic of the question. These facts, in combination with the view that semantic interpretations are determined by underlying P-markers, certainly preclude the possibility of assigning all of the sentences of (102) the same underlying P-markers. But there is still a possibility that some of the sentences of (102) may be so related — for example, b and c, or d and e.

Although certain possibilities may be suggested, it is not at all clear how to embed the description of tag, negative, and emphatic yes-no questions in the kind of syntactic and semantic analysis that is being proposed here for questions. In any event, we do not provide any account of these types in this study, and it must be borne in mind that this is an important gap in our suggested treatment of questions.

To return to simple yes-no questions, the only fact concealing their wh character is that a Sentence Adverbial constituent dominating wh is deleted when preceded by a sentence initial Q. It is worth mentioning that this is a rather recent development of the language and that at one time yes-no questions beginning with whether, like (126), did occur. Modern English can thus be looked upon as having developed in this regard simply by adding the required deletion rule (see Rule T3, p. 105). In most question cases, Q is also not manifested phonetically. But this is a general fact about English since, with one very interesting type of exception, to be discussed later, Q is always deleted. We thus treat the underlying P-markers of all questions uniformly as containing Q plus at least one not necessarily contiguous occurrence of wh. In no case does Q occur without an occurrence of wh, although the converse is not the case, since wh occurs in various nominalizations like (100), relative phrases, certain complement phrases, etc. This indicates that they are independent elements.

If one begins to think about the actual rules required to introduce wh into the underlying P-markers of English sentences, one is struck by the apparent complications involved in specifying

which constituents may dominate <u>wh</u> and thus be 'questioned'.
An enormous range of constituents may apparently be 'questioned',
including Noun Phrase or some of its subconstituents, a wide variety of adverbial constituents, etc. We believe, on the contrary,
that the range of constituents that can be 'questioned' is actually
quite small and, with one possible exception, is restricted to Noun
Phrase and probably to the Determiner constituent of Noun Phrase.
This generalization seems superficially impossible because
a multitude of distinct adverbial types can apparently be 'questioned'. But we have already provided a reason to consider these
'questioned' adverbials in the form of <u>when</u>, <u>where</u>, <u>why</u>, <u>how</u>,
etc., as cases of questioned determiner<u>s</u>. Although we have not
said so before, this treatment is inherently related to the claim
that the relevant adverbial elements are actually reduced versions of Preposition + Noun Phrase structures, this being the
general form of adverbials in English. Hence, for example,
<u>where</u> is the question form of <u>somewhere</u>, but this in turn must
be considered a reduced form of the underlying structure <u>at +</u>
<u>some + place</u>, where the occurrence of <u>place</u> is dominated <u>by</u>
Pro. We shall describe the Preposition + Noun Phrase charac-
ter of adverbials later. But it must be emphasized that this claim
is simply being presented rather than justified in detail.

The generalization that a 'questioned' constituent can only be
a Noun Phrase, or even the Determiner constituent of a Noun
Phrase, also seems impossible for those questions which contain <u>how</u> in other than Adverb$_{\text{manner}}$ occurrence, i.e., those
like <u>a-c</u> in

(103) a. how long is the car
       b. how fast does he run
       c. how often does he come
       d. the car is a somewhat long thing
       e. he runs at a somewhat fast rate
       f. he comes at somewhat frequent intervals
       g. ?the car is a thing which is long to an extent
       h. ?he runs at a rate which is fast to an extent
       i. ?he comes at intervals which are frequent to an
           extent

But there is reason to believe that these questions are also analyzable as containing a Noun Phrase dominating an occurrence
of <u>wh</u>. Hence, (103)a-c can be related to the noun phrases in
(10\overline{3})d-f, respectively. The relation between <u>how</u> and <u>somewhat</u>
seems rather clear on the basis of examples of this type alone.
Furthermore the forms in (103)d-f are themselves associated,
respectively, with (103)g-i, regardless of whether the latter are
fully grammatical or not (the question marks indicate their doubtful status in this regard). But this immediately suggests that

somewhat should be considered the automatic result of rules
needed in the grammar anyway by assuming it to have the underlying structure to + a/some + extent, where the occurrence of
extent is a Pro. In short, somewhat bears the same relation to
to some extent that someplace bears to at some place. Thus again
we posit alternate forms of a Noun that serves as the head of adverbial constituents, the alternates being differentiated by the
presence or absence of the constituent Pro. Note that the rule
required to permute somewhat around a preceding adjective need
not be added especially for this case. It will be a special instance
of the rule required to permute extremely, amazingly, etc. ,
around a preceding adjective to yield extremely stupid, amazingly stupid, etc. , from stupid to an extreme extent (degree), stupid
to an amazing extent, etc. , after the rule that has dropped the
preposition, article, and noun and added -ly to the adjective has
applied. We see then that the association of how with the wh form
of the indefinite determiner preceding a pro-form occurrence of
extent (or perhaps degree) in a quantity adverbial receives very
strong independent support. Non-manner adverbial how questions are also most adequately described as cases of 'questioned'
determiners.

   There are many other types of questions apparently incompatible
with our generalization, including those which semantically 'question' the Verb Phrase and Verb Complement like a and b in

(104) a. what did Mary do
       b. what does Mary like to do
       c. Mary did something
       d. Mary likes to do something

However, (104)a and b have a straightforward association with
(104)c and d, respectively, so that derivation from Noun Phrase,
and also Determiner structure, is well supported and provides
automatically for the form of the question word, what being the
usual wh form of the indefinite article plus the neuter pro-form
one/thing (something) in questions. We shall not argue in detail
here that these cases and others can be subsumed under our generalization.[27] Nevertheless, some further evidence for this is supplied by our discussion of nominalizations in Section 4.3.

   Although our generalization about the range of wh occurrence
in underlying P-markers is still not fully precise, it is sufficiently precise to explain why there are no question forms of prepositions, tense elements, modals, conjunctions, verbs, etc. The
Sentence Adverbial constituent, however, appears to be a much
more thoroughgoing exception to the generalization that wh is
restricted to the constituents of Noun Phrase. Although there
are a few sentence adverbials that have recognizable, though
unusual, Noun Phrase structure, such as in fact, in principle,

the basic exponents of this constituent, or at least those which
most naturally relate to yes-no questions, do not appear to have
this structure. Earlier examples suggest that the structure of
'questioned' Sentence Adverbial constituents includes the element
either-or, which occurs in disjunctions. Other evidence suggests
that yes-no questions may inherently involve disjunction with or.
It seems more likely that these questions are syntactically based
on such disjunction than that this is a purely semantic feature of
either-or. It is important that there are questions with disjunction formally like yes-no questions whose answers are not sentence adverbials, but rather in effect one term of the disjunct.
Thus in

(105) a. did John or Harry go hunting (in the sense of which
           person)

b. $\begin{Bmatrix} \text{John} \\ \text{Harry} \end{Bmatrix}$ went hunting

c. $\begin{Bmatrix} \text{John} \\ \text{Harry} \end{Bmatrix}$ did

we must answer (105)a with (105)b or c, not with yes or no. The
striking fact is that, semantically at least, ordinary yes-no questions have the same disjunctive character, which is also revealed
by the optional final disjunctive marker (or not), which they may
contain. And there are even clearer disjunctive versions:

(106) a. did John go hunting
       b. did John go hunting or not
       c. did John or did John not go hunting

These facts suggest that yes-no questions involve the request
for a specification of one of two alternatives that are in fact disjunctions of sentences. In the ordinary yes-no questions and
their variants, like (106), the sentences disjoined are apparently
a sentence S and its negation. It is then possible that yes-no questions, or more generally disjunctive questions — to include (105)a
— may be based on the generalized transformational process of
disjunction formation. Thus such question types would be strongly differentiated from the other types of questions that we have
suggested are based on 'questioned' Noun Phrase elements. The
relation of disjunctive questions to disjunctive tag questions like

(107) who came, Bill or Tom

complicates the issue further. There is another important fact
that suggests a basic differentiation between disjunctive questions
and those based on 'questioned' Noun Phrase constituents. Although a question may contain more than one constituent which
is 'questioned' by dominating wh, this is not true if one of these
constituents is Sentence Adverbial:

(108) a. *did who go home
      b. *will John see whom
      c. *can John see Bill why
      d. *did John or Bill see whom

There are thus several facts suggesting that, even if the generalization about the range of 'questionable' elements in terms of
wh distribution in a Noun Phrase can be extended to cover other
cases, still it will not hold for Sentence Adverbial. Hence, apparently there must be at best a two-part condition specifying
the distribution of question-relevant wh in underlying P-markers.

To complete the discussion, however, we must point out some
facts suggesting the opposite possibility, namely that even yes-
no and other disjunctive questions may be considered to be based
on 'questioned' Determiner constituents. We have seen that simple yes-no questions are based on 'questioned' either. But it is
striking that either does occur as a Determiner:

(109) a. I don't like either man
      b. either the statement 'John ate the meat' or the state-
          ment 'Bill ate the meat' is true
      c. either the statement 'John ate the meat' or the state-
          ment ' John did not eat the meat' is true

The clear Determiner status of either in (109)a certainly suggests the possibility that the sentence initial either, which we
have taken to be a Sentence Adverbial, may also be a Determiner.
And this could relate to disjunctive questions, perhaps through
sentences like (109)a and b. Hence, although no direct relation
can be justified at present, it is too soon to exclude the possibility that even disjunctive questions may be based on 'questioned'
Determiner constituents.

An important fact concerning the generalization about question-
relevant wh distribution just discussed for English is that it appears equally valid for other languages. This suggests the hypothesis that wh as a scope marker for Q is a universal[28] and that
it is distributed in the underlying P-markers of the sentences of
all languages by general conditions within the theory of linguistic
descriptions, namely a precise version of our rough generalization about Noun Phrase, Determiner, and perhaps Sentence Adverbial.[29] Thus we doubt that there are any particular rules in
English introducing either question-relevant wh or Q. There are,
of course, many particular rules of English restricting the occurrence of other elements with these previously introduced elements.

We do not yet know how to characterize precisely the required
universal syntactic rule for introducing wh. This will evidently
require a cross-linguistic account of such notions as Noun Phrase
and Determiner. But this task does not seem beyond the scope of

reasonable development of the present theory of transformational grammar, especially if this is taken to include certain extensions recently proposed by Chomsky (unpublished). These would include the separation of the lexicon from the phrase structure rules, which would then generate only highly abstract structures whose last lines contain dummy elements instead of actual lexical items. To complete the generation of underlying P-markers, there would be a substitution condition that replaces the dummy terminal symbols generated by the phrase structure rules with either highly structured lexical items from the dictionary (whose entries would now be P-markers of a limited type) or else other fully structured underlying P-markers. We shall not pursue here the investigation necessary to show that a universal treatment of wh and Q in these terms is possible. However, the notions necessary for this goal, which would include a substantive account of the basic constituent and relational concepts, must certainly be characterized in an adequate theory of the syntactic component on quite independent grounds. Thus we do not consider it inappropriate to suggest a semantic analysis that depends on these notions. Here, as elsewhere, the theory of the semantic component requires a very strong and highly specified theory of the syntactic component. We shall return to this observation later, where we also argue that there are strong semantic and other grounds for considering wh, Q, and other related elements as universals.

We conclude this brief discussion of the syntax of questions by describing in somewhat greater detail the actual rules required. We recognize that the following discussion does not begin to do justice to the full range of question structures in English. In particular, it says nothing about tag, emphatic, or negative questions and presupposes that wh is already distributed correctly in underlying P-markers. We believe, however, that it correctly formalizes a number of features of English questions that must be characterized by any adequate description.

It has been claimed that in the phrase structure part of the grammar Q is generated (perhaps by a universal rule) at the left of certain underlying P-markers. Then wh morphemes are attached by certain, as yet incompletely known, general conditions to certain constituents whose specification was discussed earlier. In other words, wh is attached to a constituent C just in case C is the lowest element dominating wh. In the presence of Q, more than one wh may be attached, subject to the condition about Sentence Adverbials mentioned earlier and perhaps subject also to further particular restrictions of English. However, many particular restrictions in English that seem to be required on the distribution of wh are probably not. For example, in

(110) a. *what is who
      b. *someone is something

the nonoccurrence of (110)a is not a special fact about the distribution of wh but follows automatically from the nonoccurrence
of (110)b and previous decisions about questions. Many other restrictions will no doubt have a similar treatment.

    We claim, then, that the rules of question formation (pp. 104-
105) operate on structures like those in Diagrams 4.6 and 4.7.

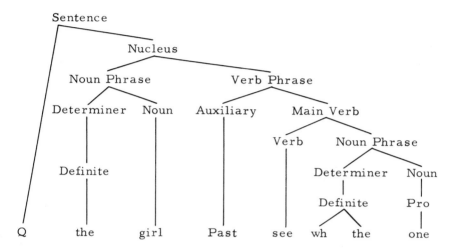

which one did the girl see

(I)

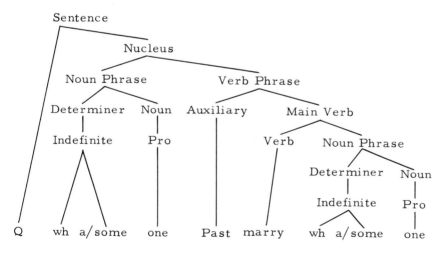

who married whom

(II)

Diagram 4.6

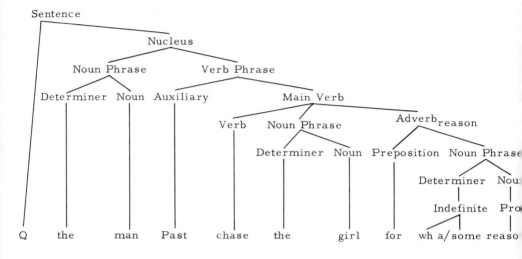

why did the man chase the girl

(I)

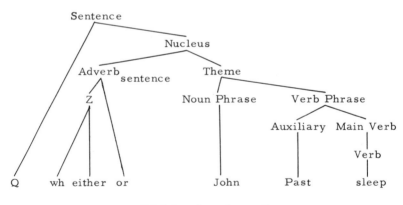

did John sleep (or not)

(II)

Diagram 4.7

For such underlying structures, at least the following ordered transformational rules are required:

(T1) # + (Q), X, Noun Phrase, Y ⟹ 1, 3, 2, 4   (optional except when
        1   2   3   4   1 does not contain Q)
      where 3 dominates a sequence which begins with wh.

(T2) # + $\underline{Q}$, X, Noun Phrase, Tense + $\left\{\begin{matrix}\text{null}\\\underline{\text{have}}\\\underline{\text{be}}\\{}_1\overline{\text{Modal}}{}_1\\{}_2\quad4\end{matrix}\right\}_2$, $\left\{\begin{matrix}\text{Verb + Y}\\\text{Y}\\5\end{matrix}\right\}_2$
     1   2 3

$\Longrightarrow$ 1, 2, 4, 3, 5 (obligatory except where 2 is a Sentence
Adverbial)

where 2 dominates $\underline{\text{wh}}$.

(T3) # + $\underline{Q}$, Sentence Adverbial, X $\Longrightarrow$ 1, null, 3 (obligatory)
     1   2   3
where 2 dominates $\underline{\text{wh}}$.

(T4) #, $\underline{Q}$, X, # $\Longrightarrow$ 1, 3, 2, 4 (obligatory)
     1 2 3 4
where 3 does not dominate a $\underline{\text{wh}}$ (except for one which is
not the leftmost element of a Relative constituent).

(T5) X, $\underline{Q}$, Y $\Longrightarrow$ 1, null, 3 (obligatory)
     1 2 3
where 3 is not equal to #.

Rule (T1) brings Noun Phrase constituents dominating $\underline{\text{wh}}$ to the
left of P-markers. It operates for relative phrases and certain
complement phrases as well as for questions. Were it not for our
assumption that all 'questioned' forms can be analyzed as either
'questioned' Noun Phrase or Sentence Adverbial constituents, the
third term of Rule (T1) would have to mention every adverbial type
that can be questioned including $\text{Adverb}_{\text{manner}}$, $\text{Adverb}_{\text{time}}$, Ad-
$\text{verb}_{\text{locative}}$, etc., making quite a large list, in order to account
for structures like

(111) a. how did he fall
      b. when did he fall
      c. where did he fall
      d. how often did he fall
      e. how quickly did he fall
      f. where did he fall to

etc. We assume, however, that the 'questioned' constituents here
are reduced versions of Prepositon + Noun Phrase structures
roughly of the form in what way, at what time, at what place, at
what intervals, at how quick a rate, and to what place, respectively. For such structures it is sufficient to move the Noun

Phrase, which was mentioned in the second term in Rule (T1),
to the far left. In the variants of (111) which actually contain the
Preposition + Noun Phrase structure, such as

(112) a. in what way did he fall
b. at what time did he fall [this is not really a variant of (111)b]
c. at what place did he fall
d. at what intervals did he fall
e. at how quick a rate did he fall
f. to what place did he fall

the preposition has been moved to the far left by a separate rule,
which we do not give even though its environment involves wh.
This rule is, of course, independently motivated (and has been
given before)[30] since the prepositions can be found unmoved:

(113) a. *what way did he fall in
b. what time did he fall at
c. what place did he fall at
d. what intervals did he fall at
e. how quick a rate did he fall at
f. what place did he fall to

Hence, Rule (T1) is not incorrect simply because it fails to mention the various types of Adverbial constituent. Since in some
cases the preposition must be moved to the left, the rule of preposition transfer with wh must be obligatory in certain cases but
otherwise does not affect our discussion. The rule of preposition
preposing is discussed further in Section 4.3.

Rule (T1) is optional in order to permit the derivation of sentences like

(114) a. when did John see whom
b. whom did John see when
c. John saw Bill where
d. John saw who yesterday

However, the c and d items here raise fundamental problems
not handled by our rules. In particular, we claim (cf. the reference in footnote 27) that such sentences are possible only when
the questioned constituent is emphasized; thus in cases of non-
emphasis Rule (T1) is obligatory. There are special intonational
facts associated with emphasis in questions, particularly the fact
that the rising intonation occurs on the emphasized questioned
constituent rather than at the end of the sentence. Hence, there
is a rise on who in d. Many other interesting and important relations between questions and emphasis require discussion, including the fact that the answer to a question with a wh-marked
constituent X must really have an answering X that is emphasized.

These facts are, however, not handled by our rules, which will require some modification when they are extended to cover cases of emphasis.

If the only element questioned by wh is the subject Noun Phrase, Rule (T1) operates vacuously, that is, the output is the same as the input since X is necessarily null (presubject elements being excluded by selection with Q). There are other necessary restrictions that have not been built into Rule (T1). For example, the rule does not prevent more than one wh-'questioned' element from being shifted to the far left and allows free combination of all such shifted elements. Yet this is not actually allowed. Various types of Noun Phrase originating in adverbials may be freely moved to the far left of P-markers containing Q, but in this case they must be conjoined with and (with the usual reduction of all but the last to comma intonation):[31]

(115) a. when, where, and how did John see Bill
       b. *when where how did John see Bill

But if a Noun Phrase whose origin is outside an Adverbial constituent is shifted to the far left, a Noun Phrase with such an origin cannot be shifted. We see the converse in

(116) a. *who where did John see
       b. *where who did John see
       c. *where and who did John see
       d. *who and where did John see

A 'questioned' object Noun Phrase can, however, be moved to the far left in the presence of a 'questioned' subject Noun Phrase:

(117) a. what did who see
       b. which boy did which girl marry

Rule (T2) provides the shift of part of the Auxiliary constituent with the preceding Noun Phrase in cases of yes-no questions and cases where a wh-'questioned' constituent has been moved to the far left between Q and the subject Noun Phrase by Rule (T1). Rule (T2) is hence the reformulation in our terms of Chomsky's T_q.[32]

The fact that our analysis of yes-no questions requires that they have a Sentence Adverbial dominating wh, plus the fact that Rule (T1) precedes Rule (T2), permits a unitary statement of Rule (T2) for such cases as

(118) a. did John go home
       b. when did John go home
       c. when did who go home

etc., and accounts for the absence of the Auxiliary shift (and subsequent obligatory insertion of do by a well-known rule) in

(119) who went home

instead of

(120) *did who go home

In (118)a, the X of Rule (T2) which dominates wh is Sentence Adverbial; in (118)b and c, the reduced Noun Phrase head of an Adverb$_{time}$ — moved to that position by application of Rule (T1). Example (118)c shows quite clearly that the absence of the Auxiliary shift in (119) is not due to the fact that the subject is 'questioned'. Thus much additional support is provided for the claim that yes-no questions have underlying P-markers with wh-'questioned' Sentence Adverbial constituents, since without this assumption no simple, unitary account of the facts concerning Auxiliary shift in such sentences as (118)-(120) would be possible.

Rule (T2) permits the derivation of two alternative forms of yes-no questions in cases where the morpheme have is a Verb.[33]

(121) a. does John have a book
       b. has John a book

Rule (T2) permits the derivation of these alternatives for have alone because only have is both a Verb and part of the Auxiliary constituent. Hence, when have is a Verb in some underlying P-marker, then that P-marker has two different bracketings which satisfy the structure index of Rule (T2), namely:

Q, X, Noun Phrase, Tense + Null, have + Y
1   2   3   4   5

and

Q, X, Noun Phrase, Tense + have, Y.[34]
1   2   3   4   5

This treatment automatically provides for the sentences of (121) and all analogous pairs being full paraphrases, because such pairs are always derived from the same underlying P-marker. Furthermore, when the rules for got are added (as mentioned in footnote 33), the semantic explanation is automatically extended to sentences like

(122) has John got a book

since this sentence and all analogous ones have the same underlying P-markers as their corresponding have sentences of (121). Hence, it follows from our assumptions about the operation of projection rules that all such cases as (121)a, (121)b, and (122) are synonymous with one another.

Rule (T2) is optional where the second term is a Sentence Adverbial in order to account for the fact that some forms of yes-no questions are without Auxiliary inversion, namely the so-called 'echo questions', like

(123) John has a book⟋

where the mark indicates rising intonation. We shall discuss the intonation later. It is not entirely clear that this mode of derivation for sentences like (123) is correct, for it appears that (123) bears the same relation to

(124) has John a book

as a bears to b in

(125) a. John had w͟h͟a͟t⟋ before he died
          b. what did John have before he died

Sentences like (125)a have also sometimes been referred to as echoes. It seems to us that the underlying difference between (125)a and b is whether or not the 'questioned' object Noun Phrase is emphasized. It is this emphasis which, we think, permits the questioned object Noun Phrase not to be moved to the far left. There is no sentence exactly like (125)a that does not have the rise on w͟h͟a͟t͟. There is, however, an alternative of (125)b that does have a rise on w͟h͟a͟t͟.

If the difference between ordinary w͟h͟-echo questions and non-echo questions is one of presence or absence of emphasis, with corresponding effects on intonation, then it seems natural that the difference between yes-no echo questions and nonecho questions should also depend on whether or not emphasis occurs. Thus the difference between (123) and (124) and between analogous types of sentences should not be due to an optional property of Rule (T2). However, there are difficulties in building this parallelism into the rules. These concern the distinctions discussed earlier between 'questioned' sentence adverbials and 'questioned' Noun Phrase. Thus, in this regard, our rules are in need of improvement.

Rule (T3) deletes a Sentence Adverbial constituent which dominates an occurrence of w͟h͟ and is preceded by Q͟. Rule (T3) thus accounts for the fact that the form w͟h͟e͟t͟h͟e͟r͟ occurs only in embedded clauses, and not in yes-no questions. Without Rule (T3) the syntactic component would generate such unacceptable strings as

(126) *whether did John go (or not)

with the same falling declarative sentence intonation as ordinary wh-questions. Rule (T3) thus 'disguises' the fact that yes-no questions are wh-questions. Unless Rule (T3) follows Rule (T2), the appropriate w͟h͟ element would not be dominated by the X of the first term of Rule (T2), and the Auxiliary permutation would not occur in yes-no questions.

Further support for this treatment of yes-no questions as con-

taining a Sentence Adverbial constituent dominating <u>wh</u> in the
presence of Q is given by complements of verbs like <u>wonder</u>.
One finds structures, like the following, in which the complements are like wh-questions except that no Auxiliary shift has
occurred:

(127) a. I wonder when John came home
       b. I wonder where John lives
       c. I wonder how John sleeps
       d. I wonder whether John sleeps

There is a Sentence Adverbial type here, namely d. But <u>wonder</u>
is a member of a class of 'parenthetical' verbs including <u>notice</u>,
<u>think</u>, etc., which can be shifted with their preceding subject and
Auxiliary to the end of the sentence. The striking thing is that
when this occurs with <u>wonder</u>, the wh-clauses are found in their
full question forms, i.e., with the Auxiliary shift:

(128) a. when did John come home, I wonder
       b. where does John live, I wonder
       c. how does John sleep, I wonder
       d. does John sleep, I wonder

and the full sentence form of the Sentence Adverbial wh-clause
contains no <u>whether</u>. But all of these facts can be explained if
we simply assume that the complements of <u>wonder</u> in these cases
are P-markers containing initial Q. Then the fact that there is
an Auxiliary shift in (128) but none in (127) follows automatically
from the fact that Rule (T2) requires Q to be in sentence initial
position, which is true only in (128). Similarly, the fact that
<u>whether</u> is dropped in (128)d but not in (127)d follows automatically,
since Rule (T3) also requires that the Sentence Adverbial follow a
sentence initial Q, which is true only in (128).

    Rule (T4) permutes the Q morpheme to the end of any P-marker
which contains no occurrence of <u>wh</u> not part of a Rel constituent,
Comp constituent, etc. Since every underlying P-marker with an
occurrence of Q must receive at least one <u>wh</u>, Rule (T4) can apply
only to structures in which a <u>wh</u> was added to a Sentence Adverbial
constituent deleted by a previous application of Rule (T3). The
presence of Q at the end of such P-markers accounts for the fact
that yes-no questions of both the echo and shifted Auxiliary types
have rising intonation, in contrast to the falling intonation of declaratives and ordinary wh-questions. In the latter cases the <u>wh</u>
morphemes are associated with constituents other than the Sentence Adverbial. In other words, we claim that the rising or question intonation is simply the way Q is spelled when it occurs in
sentence final position. Elsewhere it is always deleted by Rule
(T5).[35] That is, we assume that, unless special rules apply, every
sentence has the falling or declarative intonational pattern.

Rule (T4) is most in need of modification to take account of the
relations of questions and emphasis. Apparently it must be modified in such a way that when a wh-questioned constituent is emphasized (which must be marked by the presence of some morpheme), Q has a reflex a rising intonation at the point of that
emphasis element. This would account for the intonation in such
sentences as (114)d, which is not the usual falling intonation pattern of ordinary wh-questions, and in general for the so-called
'incredulity' intonation of echo questions. Hence, even in such
cases of emphasis we claim that all instances of rising intonation in questions are ultimately morphophonemic reflexes of the
morpheme Q. Because there are many problems in actually ex-
tending the rules to cover such cases, we have not attempted to
do so here. It is interesting, however, that the connection of Q
with rising intonation in English, which we have partially shown,
and our posited universality for Q suggest the beginnings of a
possible explanation for the sometimes claimed universality of
rising intonation in questions. This explanation could take the
form of a universal morphophonemic rule for Q.

Our analysis derives echo questions from the same underlying
P-markers as corresponding nonechoes, with the possible exception of the presence or absence of emphasis markers. It is
sometimes thought that echo questions, in particular the yes-
no varieties such as

(129) John likes bourbon

can be formed simply by adding to or changing the intonation of
the appropriate declaratives, whereas except for differences of
emphasis our description derives (129) from the same underlying
P-marker as

(130) does John like bourbon

Actually, the idea that yes-no echoes can be formed by a simple
intonation shift in declaratives is false. These echoes obey many
of the same restrictions as ordinary yes-no questions like (130):

(131)   a. *$\left\{ \begin{array}{l} \text{certainly} \\ \text{probably} \\ \text{yes} \\ \text{maybe} \end{array} \right\}$ John likes bourbon

         b. *John $\left\{ \begin{array}{l} \text{scarcely} \\ \text{hardly} \end{array} \right\}$ likes bourbon

etc. It is true that the some-any contrast shown in (81) and (82)
groups echo questions with declaratives rather than with nonecho
questions. However, this probably results in some way from
the presence of emphasis in echoes since emphasis appears
to reverse the conditions which permit unstressed some

to become <u>any</u> in questions:

    (132) a. John drank some bourbon
             b. *John drank any bourbon
             c. did John drink some bourbon
             d. did John drink any bourbon
             e. John drank some bourbon
             f. *John drank any bourbon
             g. did John drink <u>some</u> bourbon
             h. *did John drink <u>any</u> bourbon

It is true that in (132)h the emphasis is on the determiner itself,
while at best in (132)f it must be posited on the deleted 'questioned' Sentence Adverbial constituent. Thus the relation between the elimination of the possibility of introducing <u>any</u> in ordinary echo yes-no questions and emphasis is unclear. Nonetheless, there does appear to be some relation. Hence, <u>some-any</u>
facts do not really undermine the strong evidence in (131) that
yes-no echo questions must, like their nonecho variants, be derived from underlying P-markers containing Q and a <u>wh</u>-'questioned' Sentence Adverbial constituent (probably with emphasis
marker). The apparent similarity between echoes and declaratives is quite misleading, and in no sense can the former be described as being derived from the latter by mere shift in intonation.

    This completes our syntactic treatment of questions. One
general comment should be added. In earlier treatments of transformational grammar, such as Chomsky's in <u>Syntactic Structures</u>,
optional singulary transformations had at least two distinct functions. First, they derived various distinct sentence types, questions, imperatives, negatives, etc., from one underlying declarative type. They thus had a substantive role in explaining difference
in cognitive meaning between sentences of different syntactic types
and similarity in cognitive meaning between sentences of the same
syntactic type. Second, singulary transformations related optional
variants that were full paraphrases. These were intuitively stylistic variants of each other like

    (133) a. all the men are married
             b. the men are all married
             c. he found out the truth
             d. he found the truth out

In our discussion of the syntax of questions, imperatives, etc.,
we have given a great deal of support for a conception in which
only the second function of singulary transformations survives.
It therefore seems reasonable to say in general that the different
outputs produced by optional singulary transformations are merely
stylistic variants necessarily having the same cognitive meaning.

Thus there can be a uniform characterization of the function of optional rules for both the syntactic and phonological components; such rules derive what is referred to in linguistics as free varia-tion, and nothing else.

In Section 4.2.5 we shall explain how in our conception of the syntactic component a linguistic description can account for re-lations between sentence types.

Besides this fairly explicit description of the syntax of ques-tions, it is necessary to state more precisely the semantic de-scription that must accompany it. In particular, it is necessary to describe in greater detail the reading that must be assigned to Q and the function of wh, as well as the way in which the reading of Q amalgamates with other readings.

The function of Q is to indicate that the P-marker containing it underlies a question. Question-relevant occurrences of wh in a P-marker that contains Q have the function of picking out those elements in the P-marker which are 'questioned'. In other words, wh operates as a scope marker for Q. Our task now is to de-scribe how these interrelations between Q and occurrences of wh play a role in amalgamations performed by P1 and what the read-ings for a whole question are like.

Each occurrence of a question-relevant wh in an underlying P-marker is in an n-ary branching, where n is equal to or greater than 2. (See Diagram 4.8.) For each such case there is a P1 which amalgamates the readings assigned to the constituents 2 ... n (ter-minal or not) to provide a derived set of readings for the constituent C.[36] In order to formalize the scope operation of wh in such situations, we place a condition upon all P1 that requires the derived reading associated with C through the amalgamation

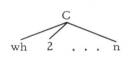

Diagram 4.8

of the readings of 2 ... n to be uniquely bracketed and labeled as a wh-bracketing. We can now describe more precisely than be-fore, but still informally, the reading of Q.

The reading of Q must formally represent the following con-ceptual content: the speaker requests that the hearer provide a true sentence one of whose readings is identical with a reading belonging to the set associated with the constituent with which the reading of Q will be amalgamated, except that any wh-bracketed substring of such a reading must have some additional semantic markers. Intuitively, we are formulating the reading of Q in such a way that it determines the set of 'possible answers' to the question that the P-marker containing Q underlies. Clearly, the semantic interpretation of a question must specify its pos-sible answers, since any speaker hearing a given question can tell what are linguistically appropriate answers. Our previous

examples of answers to questions were largely restricted to forms
that were closely related syntactically to the question they answered. These examples dealt only with answers which replaced
wh-'questioned' constituents of type C with distinct constituents
of type C. Hence, to a question like

(134)   who hit the bachelor

we considered only answers like

(135)   Harry hit the bachelor

But there are also perfectly suitable answers like:

(136)   a.   Harry hit the unmarried man
        b.   the unmarried man was hit by Harry
        c.   the man who was never married was hit by Harry

etc. In short, the notion of 'answer' must be broadened to include
paraphrases of forms that simply delete Q and replace the forms
of wh-questioned constituents by appropriate distinct constituents
of type C. A characterization of the set of possible answers for
a given question is reached by virtue of the fact that in the conceptual content of Q there is reference to the reading of an answer. All answers that are paraphrases of one another will be
included among the possible answers because they have the same
reading. The condition that the reading of an answer must have
semantic content over and above what is in the reading for the
corresponding question means that nothing is a possible answer
to a question if it is simply a sentence whose underlying P-marker
is identical to that of the question except for the absence of Q and
all occurrences of question-relevant wh. Hence, b is not an answer to a in

(137)   a.   who saw Harry
        b.   someone saw Harry

Thus the present approach to the meaning of Q explains why (137)b
is rightfully considered an evasion to the question (137)a. Our
condition on the relation between question and answer permits
indefinitely many nonparaphrase-related sentences as possible
answers to a fixed question and thus allows for the full range of
possibilities from which the truth(s) must be chosen. Hence,
among the possible answers to (137)a we find

(138)   the man who dislikes George saw Harry

(139)   I saw Harry

It is important to point out that because we have related question and answer by a semantic condition, we can explain the otherwise curious but universal fact that first- and second-person elements of all kinds alternate in question and answer. Thus if a

question contains a first-person form, the answer must contain
a corresponding second-person form, and vice versa:

(140) a.   did you see John
       b.   yes I saw John
       c.   will I be happy
       e.   yes you will be happy

etc. This kind of interchange between first-person and second-
person will follow automatically from our condition, since these
elements will have to be given readings expressing both the conceptual content of 'speaker' and 'hearer', respectively, and the fact
that the 'hearer' of one utterance may be the 'utterer' of another.
That is, the readings of first- and second-person elements will
have to permit expression of the fact that the actual referents of
such forms are contextually determined by the very use of the
sentences containing them.

The reading for Q must be roughly of this form: Q → (The
speaker requests that the hearer provide a true sentence from
the set of sentences each of which has a reading R, except that
any wh-bracketed substring of R has additional semantic markers).
The only special feature of this characterization is the symbol R,
which is a variable over readings. In order to state the projection rule that combines the reading of Q with a reading of the constituent with which it amalgamates, it is necessary to make an
explicit assumption about the character of this latter constituent.
We have assumed for simplicity that the constituent structure of
the underlying P-markers of all questions is such that Q is part
of a binary branching of the form shown in Diagram 4.9. Hence,
the semantic component must provide an amalgamation of the reading of Q with the readings
of a single constituent, Nucleus, which dominates the usual constituents, Noun Phrase and
Verb Phrase, with their constituents, etc.[37]

The projection rule which amalgamates a
reading of Nucleus with the reading for Q is
as follows:

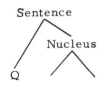

Diagram 4.9

(R2) If two given readings are associated with nodes branching
      from the same node labeled 'Sentence', one being of the form
      Q → (The speaker requests that the hearer provide a true
      sentence from the set of sentences, each of which has a
      reading R, except that any wh-bracketed substring of R
      has some additional semantic markers)

      and the other being of the form

      Lexical String → Nucleus → (m_1) → $\cdots$ → (m_k) → [1]

      there is a derived reading of the form

> Lexical String → Sentence → (The speaker requests that
> the hearer provide a true sentence from the set of sen-
> tences, each of which has a reading $(m_1) \to \cdots \to (m_k) \to$
> [X], except that any wh-bracketed substring of $(m_1) \to$
> $\cdots \to (m_k) \to$ [X] has some additional semantic markers).

This derived reading is assigned to the set of readings
associated with the node labeled 'Sentence'.

Another thing that any speaker can determine from hearing a
question is the presuppositions of the question. The notion of a
'presupposition of a question'[38] concerns a condition that the asker
of a question assumes will be accepted by anyone who tries to answer it. Thus in (137)a the asker assumes that the person who
answers will accept as a fact that someone saw Harry. Similarly,
for one of the most popular cases of presupposition, anyone who
answers

> (141) when did Harry stop beating his wife

is expected by the asker to accept as fact that Harry has been
beating his wife. Our treatment of the semantics of questions
provides a very natural formal explication for the notion 'presupposition of a question'. The presuppositons of a question are
all the sentences whose reading at the 'Sentence' node is the same
as the reading of the constituent Nucleus in the underlying P-
marker of the question (except for the syntactic marker Nucleus
and for the wh-bracketing) and all the sentences that are entailed[39]
by sentences that are presuppositions in this sense.
Thus, among the presuppositions of

> (142) when did Harry go home

> (143) where did Harry go

> (144) why did Harry go

are, respectively,

> (145) Harry went home sometime

> (146) Harry went somewhere

> (147) Harry went home for some reason

Moreover, one of the presuppositions of the question (134) is

> (148) someone hit the unmarried man

In order to complete our formalization of the two types of information that a speaker is able to get from the linguistic structure of a question, its possible answers, and its presuppositions,
we need to add two definitions to (D1) through (D5) as follows:

(D6) S is a <u>possible answer of the question</u> F if S belongs to
the set of sentences referred to in the reading assigned
to the 'Sentence' node of the leftmost semantically interpreted underlying P-marker of F.

(D7) S is a <u>presupposition of the question</u> F if S is entailed
by a sentence whose reading is identical to the reading
of the Nucleus in the leftmost semantically interpreted
underlying P-marker of F, except that there is no <u>wh</u>-
bracketing and the marker 'Sentence → Nucleus' replaces the marker 'Nucleus'.

It may be that the preceding semantic description of questions
does not apply generally in its present form because of the semantic peculiarities of yes-no questions in contrast with ordinary
wh-questions. The extent to which this is true is not easy to
determine because of our lack of knowledge of such matters as
the reading to be assigned to <u>either-or</u>. Without such a decision,
it is difficult to know whether or not the answers to yes-no questions <u>add</u> semantic markers to the reading of the Sentence Adverbial constituents of these questions. This question is related
to the problem, raised earlier, of whether and to what extent yes-
no questions must be considered to be based on syntactic disjunction. For the moment we assume that the underlying Sentence
Adverbial form of yes-no questions, namely <u>either-or</u>, is assigned a reading that permits a Nucleus dominating such a Sentence Adverbial plus a Theme to have a reading that is a paraphrase of schematically 'either Theme or not Theme'. We also
assume that Sentence Adverbial forms like <u>yes</u> and <u>no</u> contain
semantic markers specifying one or another of these semantic
alternatives so that our treatment of the relation between sentence and answer holds for yes-no questions as well as ordinary
wh-questions.

Thus, we conclude our discussion of the requirement that sentences with distinct meanings whose derivations involve only
singulary transformations have distinct underlying P-markers.
We have provided independent syntactic justification for the postulation of the morphemes Q, I, and <u>wh</u>, which differentiate and
relate the appropriate sentences in the appropriate ways and whose
readings provide in a natural way the correct semantic characterizations. The preceding apparent counterexamples to our claim
that the semantic interpretations of sentences are determined exclusively by the operation of projection rules on the sequence of
underlying P-markers in the case of sentences derived exclusively
with singulary transformations are in fact only <u>apparent</u> counterexamples.

4.2.5. <u>Relations between Sentences</u>. One further point about
elements like Q, I, <u>wh</u>, etc., must be made. An important claim

about transformational grammars is that they can explain intuitively recognized relations among sentences that cannot be characterized by constituent relations alone. Constituent relations
suffice to explain why these two sentences:

(149) John is a doctor

(150) the man who just left is a doctor

are related and how but not why (149) and

(151) is John a doctor

are related. In early statements of transformational grammar,
relations between sentences such as that between (149) and (151)
were explained by arguing that such pairs had the same underlying P-marker. But the present view of syntax and semantics
eliminates such an explanation, since (149) and (151) and all analogous sets necessarily have distinct underlying P-markers. Yet
at the same time it is necessary to explain the very real relation
between such pairs.

An alternative explanation can be offered in terms of the present
theory of linguistic descriptions. We claim that such pairs of sentences are related because their underlying P-markers are 'similar'. This notion of similarity must, of course, be made precise.
This notion cannot be made precise in the required sense if similarity between P-markers is understood as identity between them
except for a difference only in the presence or absence of a few
specified morphemes. For example, the following sentences:

(152) a. John will go home
       b. John goes home
       c. John must go home

differ only in the presence or absence of two morphemes, and yet
they are not understood to be intuitively related versions of each
other, as are actives and their corresponding passives, etc.

This raises the question of how to characterize the difference
between morphemes like those which differentiate (152)a-c and
those which differentiate (149) and (151). The only natural answer to this question is that morphemes like Q, I, Negative, Passive, wh, etc., which differentiate pairs felt to be intuitively related like (149) and (151) are universal markers specified within
the theory of linguistic descriptions; but morphemes like will,
must, etc., which differentiate sets like (152) that are not versions of one another are particular to certain languages. Thus
it can be stated in the theory of linguistic descriptions that the
'similarity' underlying intuitions of syntactic relatedness among
sets of sentences must be based either on identity of underlying
structures or on the presence of universal morphemes, like Q,
wh, Negative, etc. Such markers then serve to characterize

the range of elementary sentence types in natural language.
    However, in these terms the relation between (149) and (151)
is not so clear-cut. In our terms, (151) is not based on a P-
marker differing from that of (149) only in the presence of Q and
wh. The presence of either-or also distinguishes them. As we
suggested earlier, (151) may in fact result from the disjunction
between

(153) John is not a doctor

and (149). In these terms, (151) is no more closely related to
(149) than to (153). This seems intuitively correct. Therefore,
the direct 'sentence version' relation holds not between (149) and
(151) but rather between (151) and

(154) either John is a doctor or not

Only (154) and (151) are formally related, because their underlying P-marker sequences differ only in the presence or absence
of universal Q and wh. The intuitions an English speaker has
about the relatedness of (149) and (151) must be explained within
our conception of the syntactic component on the basis of the fact
that underlying (151) is a disjunctive structure one of whose components is the structure underlying (149). The same explanation
must apply also to the relatedness of (153) and (151).
    It should be emphasized that these sentence-type markers are
not universal in the sense that they necessarily occur in every
language. It appears, for example, that the Siouan languages
have no interrogative sentences.[40] As linguistic universals, however, they are members of the set of elements specified in the
theory of linguistic descriptions from which the vocabularies of
particular linguistic descriptions are drawn. Hence, Q is analogous to the distinctive feature of Voice, which is not necessarily
distinctive in any given language.
    The general theory will probably also specify that each such
universal morpheme have associated with it an obligatory singulary transformation whose operation is signaled by that morpheme.
The description just given can be extended in the obvious way to
cover relatedness among sentences whose derivations involve
generalized transformations, but we shall not discuss this exten-
sion here.
    We should emphasize that the universality of the elements Q,
I, wh, Negative, etc., is not postulated in an ad hoc manner to
explain relatedness among sentences. But this postulation is independently motivated by semantic considerations, primary among
which is the fact that each of these elements has the same meaning
in every language in which it occurs. If such elements were not
taken to be universals, redundant specifications of the meaning
of each such element would be required in the semantic component

of almost every linguistic description, thus complicating these
descriptions and missing the obvious generalization.[41]

4.3 Apparent Counterexamples in the Case of Generalized Transformations

We have considered apparent counterexamples in sentences derived exclusively with singulary transformations. None of these
was found to be a genuine counterexample to the claim that the
semantic interpretations of sentences are determined uniquely
by the operation of projection rules on the sequence of underlying
P-markers. To complete the defense of our general thesis, we
must now consider apparent counterexamples involving generalized transformations. It must be shown that the semantic interpretation of a sentoid whose T-marker contains generalized transformations is the semantic interpretation of the sequence of underlying P-markers in this T-marker.

One type of apparent counterinstance to this claim would be a
case where at least one of the generalized transformations must
be interpreted as contributing a portion of the meaning of the sentence, i.e., where there is an element of meaning that comes
from neither the syntactic structure of the sequence of underlying
P-markers nor the lexical items they contain but is contributed
by the transformation or transformations that combine them. An
apparent counterexample of this type is the case discussed by
Chomsky of the syntactically ambiguous sentence:

(155) they found the boy studying in the library[42]

On one term of this ambiguity, studying in the library is a complement to the verb, while on the other it is a slightly deformed
relative phrase, with who is deleted, and thus a modifier of the
boy. This is shown by the fact, noted by Chomsky, that there
are two different passives:

(156) the boy studying in the library was found by them

and

(157) the boy was found by them studying in the library

Chomsky sought to account for this ambiguity on the grounds that
it results from different transformational developments of the
same kernel strings, i.e., the same pair of underlying P-markers
Thus, on his account, both terms have the P-markers in Diagram
4.10 underlying them.

But is is clear that in relation to a syntactic component that
provides constituents Rel and Comp for underlying P-markers,[44]
the underlying P-markers for the terms of ambiguity in (155) are
not those in Diagram 4.10, but rather those in Diagrams 4.11 and
4.12. Diagram 4.11 represents the case where studying in the

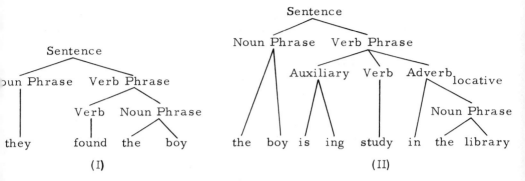

Diagram 4.10

(I) same as in Diagram 4.10 (I)

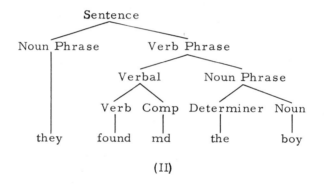

Diagram 4.11

(I) same as in Diagram 4.10 (I)

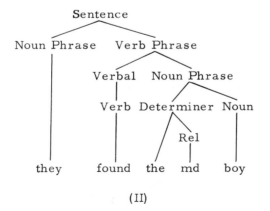

Diagram 4.12

library is a complement, Diagram 4.12 the case where it is a relative phrase. Thus the underlying P-markers for the two terms
of the ambiguity of (155) are found to differ in just the way they are
ambiguous and in just the way required for projection rules to provide the correct readings by operating on the sequence of underlying P-markers alone. This case is therefore not a counterinstance but rather a piece of supporting evidence for the position
we are defending.

One of the most interesting apparent counterexamples to the position being defended here is another case discussed by Chomsky,[42]
namely examples like

(158) I dislike John's driving

This sentence is structurally ambiguous between a 'factive' sense
and a 'manner' sense. That is to say, (158) can mean either that
the speaker dislikes the fact that John drives or that the speaker
dislikes the way in which John drives. Ambiguities between factive and manner senses have been explained by deriving the ambiguous sentence in two different ways from the same underlying
P-markers with different generalized transformations. In order
not to count these ambiguous nominalizations as counterexamples
to our position, we must show that such an explanation for cases
like (158) is incorrect.

In such cases of structurally ambiguous nominals, we must be concerned with a number of contrasting patterns of nominalization.[46]
Corresponding to almost any declarative sentence is a nominal
in which the subject of the declarative has an added genitive marker and the verb suffix is replaced by -ing. Thus, we have these
patterns:

(159) a. (i)   John washes the car
           (ii) John's washing the car
       b. (i)   John sleeps
           (ii) John's sleeping
       c. (i)   John is big
           (ii) John's being big
       d. (i)   John has three heads
           (ii) John's having three heads
       e. (i)   the book costs five dollars
           (ii) the book's costing five dollars
       f. (i)   John grows strong
           (ii) John's growing strong
       g. (i)   John wishes to live
           (ii) John's wishing to live

etc. The nominals in (159) have the factive sense of (158). The
factive sense of the ambiguity discussed by Chomsky is thus based
on nominals like (159)(ii), formed with either intransitive verbs

or transitive verbs (like <u>drive</u>, <u>eat</u>, but not <u>annoy</u>) whose object
Noun Phrase can be deleted.

There is also a quite different nominalization pattern contrasting
in several ways with that illustrated in (159). This nominalization
pattern is marked, in one version, by the presence of <u>of</u>:

(160) a.   (i)   John's washing of the car
            (ii) this washing of the car of John's
      b.   (i)   John's sleeping
            (ii) this sleeping of John's
      c.   - - - - -
      d.   - - - - -
      e.   - - - - -
      f.   - - - - -
      g.   - - - - -

Besides the presence of <u>of</u>, the second construction has several
features that differentiate it from (159). First, as illustrated by
the blanks in (160), the verbs that can occur in the second construction are far more limited. In the second construction, <u>be</u>,
<u>have</u>, middle verbs like <u>weigh</u>, <u>cost</u>, etc., copulative verbs, and
verbs with complements cannot occur, although they do in the
first. The verbs which occur in the second construction appear
to be those which can occur with manner adverbials, i.e., those
which generally have the form Adjective + <u>ly</u>, like <u>quickly</u>. This
is a crucial property of the second construction, to which we shall
return later. This fact relates to another important difference between the construction with <u>of</u> and the one without, namely that the
latter but not the former occurs with adjectives, and in fact just
those adjectives which form manner adverbials:

(161) a.   (i)   John's rapid washing of the car
            (ii)   John washes the car rapidly
      b.   (i)   this deep sleeping of John's, John's deep sleeping
            (ii)   John sleeps deeply
      c.   (i)   *John sleeps yellowly
            (ii)   *this yellow sleeping of John's
            (iii) *John's yellow sleeping

but

(162) *John's rapid washing the car

etc. Another difference between the two productive patterns
being considered is that while the first is always formed with
the verbal suffix <u>-ing</u>, the second is formed with a suffix which
has been called <u>NML</u> by Lees[47] and which has a variety of
shapes only one of which is <u>-ing</u>. The others include null/<u>-tion</u>/
<u>-ment</u>/<u>-al</u>, etc., as in

(163) a. ⎧ John's claim   ⎫
       b. ⎪ John's dramatization ⎪
       c. ⎨ John's arrangement   ⎬ (of the crime)
       d. ⎪ John's refusal   ⎪
       e. ⎩ John's proof   ⎭

etc. Ambiguity between the first and second types of construction results only when the form of NML is -ing.[48] Thus compare

(164) John's driving

which is ambiguous, with

(165) a. John's bluffing
       b. John's bluff

each of which has one of the senses found in (164). Thus (165)a
refers to the fact that John bluffs, (165)b to the way that John
bluffs.

However, the situation is complicated by the fact that the second construction is itself systematically ambiguous for a wide
range of cases. This ambiguity is revealed quite clearly by the
following examples:

(166) a. (i)   John's bluff was hurried and ineffective
           (ii) John's bluff was called
       b. (i)   John's proof of the theorem was hurried
           (ii) John's proof of the theorem was on the black-
                 board

In (166)(ii) one finds the 'object' sense, in (166)(i) the 'manner'
sense. Thus (166)b refers not only to the way in which John bluffs
but also to the abstract object which results. The 'object' sense
is associated with the possibility of occurrence of the plural morpheme:

(167) a. John's proofs
       b. John's refusals

etc. On the other hand, cases of the second construction with no
'object' sense cannot occur with the plural:

(168) a. John's handling of the crowd
       b. *John's handlings

We provide no account or explanation of the 'object' sense of the
class of second-construction nominals. We point out its existence
only to clarify the discussion of the manner sense.

It is clear then that the first construction, which has a factive
interpretation, and the second, which has a manner interpretation,
exhibit a number of important syntactic differences. In the past,[49]
these cases have been handled by special generalized transformations, one to produce each type. Thus there would be one rule

to produce the forms of (159)(ii) from structures underlying (159)(i)
and another to produce (160)(i) from structures underlying other
declaratives. Certain minor singulary rules are then also needed.

This mode of derivation ignores, however, a wide range of crucial facts about the constructions being discussed. First, it must
be emphasized that the 'manner' construction being considered
here is a special case of a much more general pattern illustrated
by the following far from complete list:

(169) a.   (i)   John's way of driving
              (ii) *the way of John's driving
              (iii) *John's driving way
              (iv) The way $\left\{\begin{array}{l}\text{in which}\\\text{that}\\\text{null}\end{array}\right\}$ John drives
              (v)   John's driving
              (vi) John drives in that way
       b.   (i)   John's manner of driving
              (ii) the manner of John's driving
              (iii) John's driving manner
              (iv) the manner in which John drives
              (v)   John's driving
              (vi) John drives in that manner
       c.   (i)   John's reason for driving
              (ii) the reason for John's driving
              (iii) *John's driving reason
              (iv) the reason $\left\{\begin{array}{l}\text{for which}\\\text{that}\\\text{why}\\\text{null}\end{array}\right\}$ John drives $\begin{array}{l} \\ \text{----------- for}\\ \\ \end{array}$
              (v)   -----
              (vi) John drives for that reason
       d.   (i)   John's purpose in driving
              (ii) the purpose of John's driving
              (iii) *John's driving purpose
              (iv) the purpose $\left\{\begin{array}{l}\text{for which}\\\text{that}\\\text{null}\end{array}\right\}$ John drives $\begin{array}{l} \\ \text{----------- for}\\ \text{----------- for}\end{array}$
              (v)   -----
              (vi) John drives for that purpose
       e.   (i)   *John's place of driving
              (ii) the place of John's driving
              (iii) John's driving place
              (iv) the place $\left\{\begin{array}{l}\text{in which}\\\text{that}\\\text{where}\\\text{null}\end{array}\right\}$ John drives $\begin{array}{l} \\ \text{----------- in}\\ \\ \end{array}$
              (v)   -----

(vi) John drives $\left\{\begin{array}{l} \text{in} \\ \text{at} \\ \text{on} \\ \text{etc.} \end{array}\right\}$ that place

f. (i)   John's period of driving
    (ii) the period of John's driving
    (iii) John's driving period
    (iv) the period $\left\{\begin{array}{l} \text{during which} \\ \text{that} \\ \text{when} \\ \text{null} \end{array}\right\}$ John drives

    (v)   - - - - -
    (vi) John drives during that period

g. (i)   John's hour of driving
    (ii) the hour of John's driving
    (iii) John's driving hour
    (iv) the hour $\left\{\begin{array}{l} \text{during which} \\ \text{that} \\ \text{when} \\ \text{null} \end{array}\right\}$ John drives

    (v)   - - - - -
    (vi) John drives during that hour

h. (i)   John's amount of driving
    (ii) the amount of John's driving
    (iii) *John's driving amount
    (iv) the amount $\left\{\begin{array}{l} \text{which} \\ \text{that} \\ \text{null} \end{array}\right\}$ John drives

    (v)   - - - - -
    (vi) John drives that amount

i. (i)   John's degree of struggle
    (ii) the degree of John's struggle
    (iii) *John's struggle degree
    (iv) the degree $\left\{\begin{array}{l} \text{to which} \\ \text{that} \\ \text{which} \\ \text{null} \end{array}\right\}$ John struggles

    (v)   - - - - -
    (vi) John struggles to that degree

j. (i)   John's extent of driving
    (ii) the extent of John's driving
    (iii) *John's driving extent
    (iv) the extent $\left\{\begin{array}{l} \text{that} \\ \text{to which} \\ \text{null} \end{array}\right\}$ John drives

    (v)   - - - - -
    (vi) John drives to that extent

Each of the sets of examples a through k in (169) reveals a
pattern of complex Noun Phrase formation based upon a noun pos-
sessing the possibility of occurrence with a preceding preposition
as the head of some Adverb constituent (except amount, whose
Preposition is, we claim, deleted). Hence, in (169)a and b, we
find manner and way serving as the heads of manner adverbials;
in c and d, reason and purpose serving as the head of purpose
adverbials; in e, place serving as the head of locative adverbials;
in f and g, period and hour serving as the heads of time adverbials;
and in h, i, and j, respectively, amount, degree, and extent serving as heads of quantity adverbials. There are many other nouns
that can function in adverbials in this way, and for such nouns we
can find sets of examples such as those in (169). For nouns that
do not have this function in adverbials, however, we cannot find
sets of examples of the appropriate kind. Thus, for two such nouns,
gun and aspect, we find

(170) a.   (i)   *John's gun of driving
             (ii) *the gun of John's driving
             (iii) *John's driving gun
             (iv) *the gun $\left\{ \begin{array}{l} \text{that} \\ \text{in which} \\ \text{for which} \end{array} \right\}$ John drives
             (v)   - - - - -
             (vi) *John drives $\left\{ \begin{array}{l} \text{in} \\ \text{for} \end{array} \right\}$ that gun
       b.   (i)   *John's aspect of driving
             (ii) *the aspect of John's driving[50]
             (iii) *John's driving aspect
             (iv) *the aspect that John drives
             (v)   - - - - -
             (vi) *John drives $\left\{ \begin{array}{l} \text{for} \\ \text{in} \end{array} \right\}$ that aspect

In (169) every set possesses at least one nominal of type (iv), and
at least one of the types (i)-(iii), as well as a full sentence with
the appropriate Noun as a head of an Adverbial constituent. The
nominals of the various types are all paraphrases within the set.
These facts suggest that all the nominals of a set are grammati-
cally related as well as related to a full sentence of type (vi),
which contains an Adverbial constituent.
   Obviously, the crucial nominals for the derivation are those of
type (iv), at least one of which is always grammatical for all the
different types. These reveal most clearly the underlying structure. They usually have alternatives with a preposition, with a
special adverbial word, with which and that, or with null. The
possibility of a special adverbial word in type (iv) correlates quite
clearly with the possibility of a single-word question form for that

type of adverbial. Hence, one finds the place where but no analogous form for extent or amount. Correlated with this, one finds
where as an interrogative form along with at what place, but for
extent and amount the only indefinite interrogatives are to what
extent and what amount. We shall explain this fact by claiming
that the nouns which form the heads of the Adverbial constituents
way, place, extent, etc., are not necessarily pro-forms. However, a few of them have, at least in some environments, both
pro-form and non-pro-form instances. Only these forms have
the single-word variants in where, when, etc.

Let us examine the other alternatives in type (iv) nominals. It
is important that, except for the null alternative, there is a similar possibility in questions for a particular type of adverbial. (This
will be clearer if it is noted that that is the form of what occurring
directly after a noun.) Thus consider the set in (169)e which corresponds to the question alternatives:

(171) a. at which place does John drive
       b. at what place does John drive
       c. where does John drive
       d. which place does John drive at
       e. what place does John drive at
       f. where does John drive at

Earlier we argued that for a number of pro-forms, including
especially those which served as the noun heads of Adverbial constituents, there were nearly identical non-pro-forms. Examples
(169) and (171) show that this assumption can also help explain
facts about non-question uses of these adverbial nouns. These
examples plus analogous ones also suggest strongly that the relevant adverbial expressions are actually reduced instances of underlying Preposition + Noun Phrase structures. Hence, the locative adverbials of (171) are based, respectively, on underlying
structures like those shown in Diagram 4.13. The structure in
4.13(III) will automatically reduce to the structure at + where by
virtue of the rule which adjoins an indefinite article to a following
pro-form, which is needed to generate someone, something, etc.,
as we pointed out earlier. With the kind of derivation suggested
by Diagram 4.13, it follows that the single-word adverbial question forms where, when, etc., can be easily embedded in a generation of adverbials as Preposition + Noun Phrase structures.
There is one further rule needed, namely that which deletes a
preposition before an indefinite article (containing wh or not)
when it has been adjoined to a pro-form. This will yield somewhere, sometime, somehow, etc., instead of the nonexistent
*at somewhere, *at sometime, *in somehow, etc. Of course,
the same rule will account for the absence of a preposition in
(171)c and all analogous cases based on adverbial pro-forms other
than place/where/there.

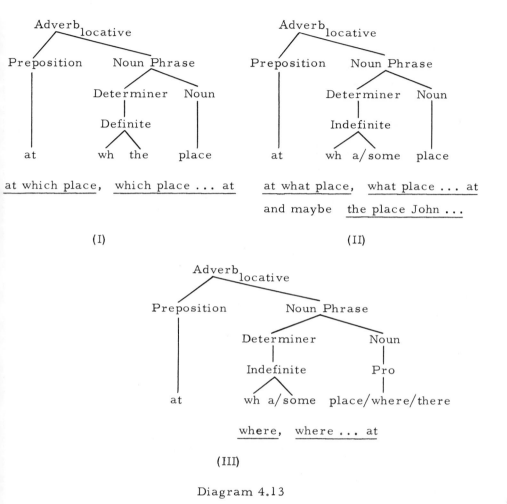

Diagram 4.13

It is important that occurrences of <u>wh</u> are found not only in structures underlying questions but also in those underlying relative phrases. This fact, plus the parallelism between the alternations in (169)(iv) and those in questions based on Adverb constituents, suggests that nominals of the form (169)(iv) are actually relative phrases derived by the well-known relative transformation.

Strong support for such an analysis comes from the observation that the relative transformation is a generalized transformation which combines two P-markers subject to a condition of noun sharing. That is, the two P-markers to be combined must share nouns which are identical not only terminally but also in higher-order constituent structure. But it is easily seen that this con-

dition of noun identity immediately relates nominals of type (iv)
to sentences of type (vi) in (169) and accounts for the deviance of
(170). In short, it seems clear that type (iv) nominals are derived
by the relative transformation, which is independently motivated
in the strongest possible way. Thus we claim that a nominal like
the first in (169)a(iv) is derived from the pair of P-markers shown
in Diagram 4.14.

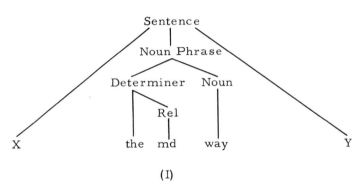

(I)

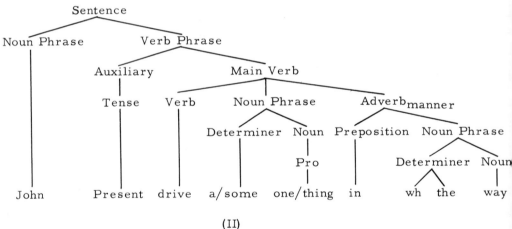

(II)

Diagram 4.14

Rule (T1), given earlier in our discussion of questions, moves
a Noun Phrase dominating wh to the front or far left (except for
Q) of a P-marker. Hence, the Noun Phrase of the Adverb$_{manner}$
constituent is so moved in Diagram 4.14(II). There is another rule,
briefly mentioned in the discussion of interrogatives, which shifts
a preposition to the far left, as it were, to join its following Noun
Phrase which has been moved by Rule (T1):

(172) a. in what place did John work
       b. in which place did John work

    c. what place did John work in
    d. which place did John work in
    e. the place which John worked in
    f. the place that John worked in
    g. the place in which John worked
    h. *the place in that (what) John worked
    i. the place John worked

This yields (172)a, b, and g as well as (172)c, d, e, and f. However, evidently this rule of preposition shift must be restricted
in relatives, unlike interrogatives, to the case where the Noun
Phrase which it joins has a Definite Determiner constituent. Otherwise, if the preposition shift is to be allowed freely in relatives
as in interrogatives, nonexistent forms like (172)h must be taken
to underlie forms like (172)i. At any rate, in the derivation we
are considering the relative rule applies, substituting the P-marker
which results from the application of Rule (T1) and the preposition
shift rule on the P-marker in Diagram 4.14(II) for the md occurrence in Diagram 4.14(I). This yields a derived Noun Phrase in
the matrix with a structure like that shown in Diagram 4.15(I).
To this structure the obligatory rule that shifts the Rel constituent
to the right of the main Noun is then applied, yielding the structure in Diagram 4.15(II). Finally, to this is applied the equally
obligatory rule which deletes the repeated noun, i.e., which operates on Determiner + Noun$_a$ + wh + Article + Noun$_a$ to delete
the second instance of Noun$_a$. This yields the structure in 4.15(III).
    There is an analogous derivation for each type (iv) nominal. The
differences between the different kinds of type (iv) nominals are
attributed to the distinction between definite and indefinite articles
(Preposition + which versus that) and to the presence or absence
of the constituent Pro (where versus place that, place in which)
in ways we indicated earlier. These derivations of type (iv) nominals require no rules or additions to the grammar that are not
required by facts quite independent of the nominal constructions
we are considering.
    There are, of course, some problems and irregularities in the
structures and derivations involved in the present analysis of nominals like (169)(iv) from P-markers like those in Diagram 4.14.
These involve restrictions that must be built into the rules that
generate underlying P-markers, as well as into various transformational rules. Such restrictions concern the whole range of
parallelisms between interrogative forms, relative forms, and
free adverbial forms. Thus a very incomplete illustration of the
contrastive facts involved is given by

(173) I. Free Adverbial
        a. indefinite
            (i) somehow
            (ii) somewhere

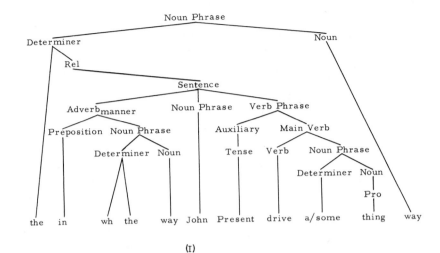

(I)

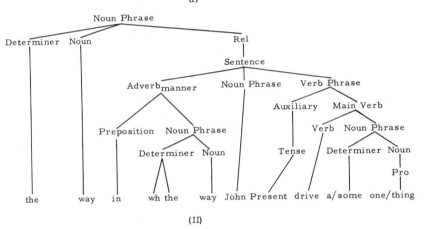

(II)

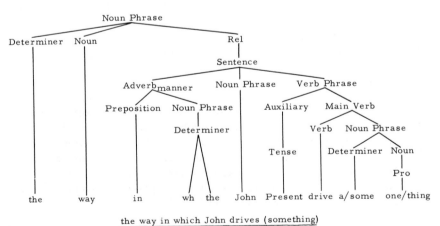

the way in which John drives (something)

(III)

Diagram 4.15

        (iii)   sometime
        (iv)   *somereason (*somewhy)
        (v)   somewhat
    b. definite
        (i)   so? (relation unclear)
        (ii)   there — here
        (iii)   then — now
        (iv)   thus? (relation unclear)
        (v)   -----

II. Relative
    a. indefinite
        (i)   the way that (*how)
        (ii)   the place where
        (iii)   the time when
        (iv)   the reason why (*the purpose why)
        (v)   *the extent how
    b. definite
        (i)   the way in which
        (ii)   the place in which
        (iii)   the time at which
        (iv)   the reason for which
        (v)   the extent to which

III. Interrogative
    a. indefinite
        (i)   how ...
        (ii)   where ...
        (iii)   when ...
        (iv)   why ...
        (v)   how ...
    b. definite
        (i)   which way
        (ii)   which place
        (iii)   which time
        (iv)   which reason, which purpose
        (v)   which extent

We claim that the general kinds of contrasting structures revealed by (173), plus earlier examples of nominals and interrogatives, can be represented by the contrasting underlying P-marker shown in Diagram 4.13 and Diagram 4.16, where we have chosen locative adverbials for the example.

Thus the present analysis associates <u>somewhere</u>, <u>where</u>, <u>the place where</u> with an adverbial noun which is a Pro, in contrast to <u>at some place</u>, <u>at what place</u>, <u>the place that ... at</u>, which are based on an adverbial noun which is not a Pro. The definite-indefinite contrast carries over. Following a suggestion of M. Geiss,[51] however, we have associated the <u>somewhere</u>, <u>there</u>, <u>here</u>

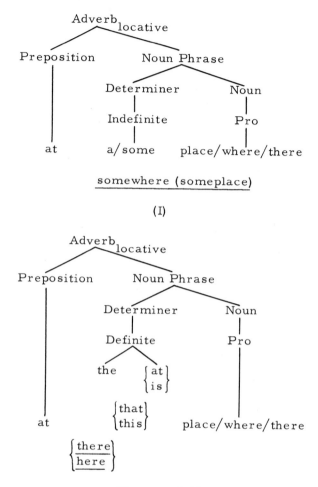

somewhere (someplace)

(I)

Diagram 4.16

and sometime, then, now distinctions with the difference between
a/some, that, and this. Our analysis then requires a number of
restrictions to be built into the part of the grammar which enumerates underlying P-markers. Only some of the adverbial nouns
must have Pro versions, and only some of the Pro-version adverbial nouns can occur after this or that in order to account for
the absence of a three-way contrast with way, reason, etc. Similarly, we must ensure that Preposition + the + Pro does not generally occur, although Preposition + the + Rel + Pro does occur,
as does Preposition + wh + the + Pro, as in Diagram 4.14(II). Moreover, some adverbial nouns with Pro versions will have them only
in some environments. In particular, reason seems to occur as
a Pro only in the presence of a preceding article that dominates
wh. Hence, the reason why in relatives, why he came in com-

plements, why in questions, all involve an attached wh on the determiner preceding the pro-form reason. But there is no *some-
why, where the determiner is without wh, and similarly no free
single-word definite adverbials analogous to then, here, etc.,
based on reason. Other restrictions for these adverbial forms
will also, no doubt, be required in the phrase structure part of
the grammar.

One of the great virtues of the present analysis of forms based
on adverbial nouns is that it accounts for the single-word character
of the free adverbial like somewhere, the relative like where,
and the interrogative like where, all with the same rule which attaches an indefinite article to the following pro-form. In the derivation of the appropriate relatives, like the place where he lives,
which is analogous to that shown for way adverbials in Diagrams
4.14 and 4.15, the application of this attachment rule will precede
the rule that drops the noun of a relative phrase which is identical
to the noun modified by the relative phrase. Hence, the structure
in Diagram 4.17(I) becomes that in 4.17(II), and this change will
occur before the deletion rule for identical nouns applies. But
then the latter rule cannot apply, since the Noun constituent place
is not identical to the Noun constituent wh + a/some + place, and
since there is no intervening Determiner constituent as the rule
requires. Notice also that the rule of attachment of indefinite
determiner to the following noun must be expanded in range to allow attachment within relatives of indefinite articles to non-pro-
forms to yield such phrases as the house where.

Furthermore, the rule which attaches indefinite articles to following pro-forms must be extended to definite articles as well
(perhaps including demonstratives). This would account for the
single-word character of then, there, now, etc. This definite-
article attachment may be rather general and may be the origin
of it, which is seen as the definite parallel to indefinite something,
perhaps as the origin of this and that in occurrences without a following noun, and perhaps even as the origin of he, she, they, etc.
But there are many detailed restrictions here. For example,
which one is two words, not one, so that the proposed attachment
cannot occur when the definite is preceded by wh although indefinite
attachment must occur. It seems, however, that there is a fairly
uncomplicated rule to drop a certain class of prepositions before
nouns which are composed of attached determiners plus pro-
forms, i.e., to drop the preposition to yield pro-form somewhere, here, there (but note to there, since then, etc.) versus
non-pro-form at some place, at this place, at that place.

Although many details must be worked out, the rules required
for converting the underlying forms of our adverbial analysis into
the occurring terminal forms are rather general. None of them
appears to be restricted in operation to the kind of adverbial nom-

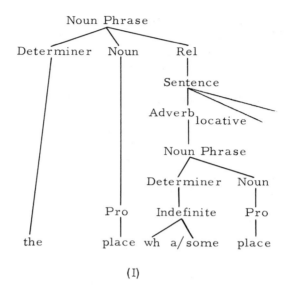

(I)

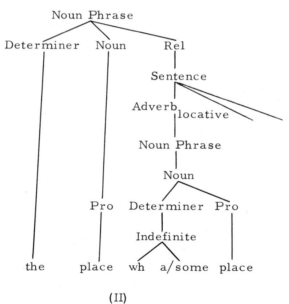

(II)

Diagram 4.17

inalizations we are discussing. Thus, the suggested treatment is, to this extent, independently justifiable.

Our next task is to suggest how the nominals of types (i)-(iii) and (v) in (169) may be derived. Type (v) nominals are of the form originally discussed by Chomsky. We have listed a sequence for type (v) only when such a sequence is a paraphrase of another

sequence in the given set. Hence, there are type (v) strings only
in sets a and b.

We claim that the nominals of types (i)-(iii) are obtained by
deriving type (ii) nominals from those of type (iv). This is accomplished by application of an optional rule which replaces a
Determiner constituent dominating <u>wh</u> (and deletes a preceding
preposition if there is one) by <u>of</u> when this determiner is the leftmost element in a Rel constituent (subject to many restrictions
as to Verb of the relativized sentence and Noun modified by the
relative phrase). This rule also adds the genitive formative to
the right of the Noun Phrase that immediately follows the Determiner constituent dominating <u>wh</u>. Hence, the optional rule we
are discussing would apply to the P-marker in Diagram 4.15(III)
and derive the P-marker shown in Diagram 4.18.

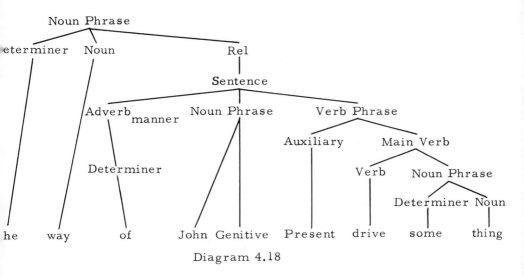

Diagram 4.18

There is a subsequent obligatory rule which replaces the Present Tense marker by -ing or NML (depending on the further environment) in the environment genitive-----.[52] An optional rule
later deletes the object of <u>drive</u>. This completes the derivation
of the nominals of form (169)(ii). The sole apparatus that must
be added to the grammar to account for this derivation, namely
the rule deriving the P-markers like Diagram 4.18 from those
like Diagram 4.15(III) (henceforth 'T_{of}'), is needed on quite other
grounds, chiefly to derive the genitive. Thus there must be a
rule to derive

(174) *the house of John's[53]

from the structure underlying

(175) the house which John has

since the internal selectional restrictions are essentially identical in the set of such pairs. But the required rule is T_{of}.

Thus we have shown how type (ii) nominals may be derived from type (iv) nominals by rules that are almost entirely independently motivated and are also quite simple. Type (iv) nominals are, in turn, derived from full sentences by the well-known relative rule. Type (i) nominals may then be easily derived from those of type (ii) by an optional rule that substitutes the Noun Phrase constituent dominating the Genitive for the article the preceding the main Noun. This rule, $T_{gen\ sub}$, would then operate on Diagram 4.18 to yield the P-marker of Diagram 4.19.

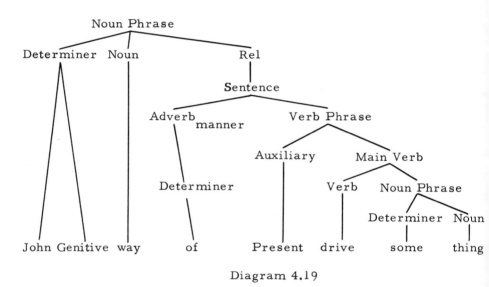

Diagram 4.19

The rule required here is also essentially independently motivated, since it is needed at least in the genitive construction to derive

(176) John's house

from the structure underlying (174). This description of the genitive accounts for the fact that one finds

(177) a house of John's

etc.,[54] in contrast to the impossible (174).

It should be emphasized here that the rules given for deriving type (i), (ii), and (iv) nominals are quite general in that they hold for the full class of nouns that serve as the heads of Adverbial constituents. The nouns way and manner are simply special cases of this set of nouns. However, the general rules for all the other cases apparently break down with these two nouns, since the type (ii

nominals for these manner words are impossible. Clearly, it is
best to account for this fact without disturbing the highly general
and simple character of the description given so far. We can
easily accomplish this by adding a rule that operates on structures
like Diagram 4.18 to substitute the Auxiliary + Verb for the noun
<u>way</u> or <u>manner</u>. Thus we add a rule that operates on the struc-
ture index:

$$X, \begin{Bmatrix} \underline{\text{way}} \\ \underline{\text{manner}} \end{Bmatrix}, \text{ of, Noun Phrase, Auxiliary + Verb, } Y$$

$$1 \quad\; 2 \qquad\qquad 3 \quad 4 \qquad\qquad 5 \qquad 6$$

and which substitutes the fifth term for the second. This rule
when applied to a structure like Diagram 4.18 will yield the structure shown in Diagram 4.20.

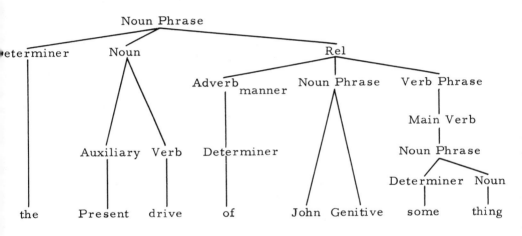

Diagram 4.20

But now if we add the restriction that $T_{gen\ sub}$ is obligatory where
the Noun dominates Auxiliary + Verb, this structure underlies one
term of the ambiguous <u>John's driving</u>. There is reason to believe
that this restriction will be needed independently in the syntactic
component.

   In short, we account for the absence of type (ii) nominals with
<u>way</u> and <u>manner</u> by utilizing these quite generally generated but
nonexistent forms as the basis for a distinct kind of nominal containing no explicit noun of the type that serves as head for Adverbials. In this way the general rules that automatically yield
type (ii) nominals are preserved, and <u>John's driving</u> is generated.
The latter must, of course, be accomplished by any syntactic component. In other words, <u>John's driving</u> and analogous forms fill
otherwise blank positions or gaps in the set of type (ii) nominals
generated by independently motivated rules. Deriving such nom-

inals from type (ii) nominals based on <u>way</u> or <u>manner</u>, instead
of by a special generalized transformation as in the past, thus
adds significantly to the simplicity of the syntactic component.

It is important that the derivation of nominals like <u>John's driv-</u>
<u>ing</u> (<u>John's cooking of the meat</u>, etc.) from nominals containing
<u>way</u> or <u>manner</u> provides an automatic explanation for the peculi-
arities, noted earlier, of the second or 'manner' construction.
The fact that such nominals may be based only on verbs co-occurri
with manner adverbials is an automatic consequence, since we have
derived them from underlying P-markers containing manner adver
bials. Schematically,

(178) John's flying of the plane was erratic

comes from <u>the Rel way was erratic</u> and <u>John flies the plane in</u>
<u>wh the way</u>. Since there are no analogues to the latter structure
with <u>be</u>, <u>have</u>, middle verbs, etc., these verbal elements can
never appear as the basis of manner nominals, with the derivation we have described. Moreover, the fact that adjectives may
occur with the nominals of the second construction, i.e.,

(179) John's foolish flying of the plane

follows automatically, since the nouns <u>way</u> and <u>manner</u> occur with
adjectives:

(180) the foolish way in which John flies the plane

Hence, the occurrence of these adjectives is automatic after the
Auxiliary + Verb sequence has replaced <u>way</u> or <u>manner</u> if they
were present before this replacement. More significantly, there
is an immediate explanation for the fact that the set of adjectives
which occurs in the manner construction is exactly that which occurs with <u>way</u> and <u>manner</u> (and moreover exactly that set which
combines with <u>-ly</u> to form manner adverbials). Thus there are
no nominals like

(181) *John's green driving of the car

because there is no nominal of the form

(182) *the green way in which John drives the car

However, the fact that the set of manner adverbials of the form
Adjective + **ly** contains just those adjectives which can co-occur
with <u>way</u> has never been explained for <u>full sentences</u> in any previous description of English. That is, there is no explanation of
why there is no sentence such as

(183) *John sleeps yellowly

But this follows directly from the absence of

(184) *John sleeps in a yellow way

if manner adverbials of the form Adjective + ly are derived, as we now suggest, from those of the form in + Determiner + Adjective + way, manner adverbials of the latter form necessarily being generated (with their adjective-way co-occurrence restrictions) by the syntactic component of English in any event. Together with our description of the second or 'manner' nominal, this explanation of the restriction on adjectives in the Adjective + ly construction in full sentences immediately explains why the adjectives occurring in the second nominal construction are just those occurring before -ly in manner adverbials, both sets being determined by co-occurrence with way. Notice the relation between this derivation of manner adverbials and our generalization about the distribution of wh in questions given earlier. Here is very strong evidence that Noun Phrase elements underlie manner adverbials.

We have provided in some detail a highly justified derivation for the ambiguous nominals being discussed from underlying structures containing the noun way or manner. This, however, provides an explanation only for one of the two senses.

Consider now the factive sense. We maintain that the first nominal construction, the one typically without of, is a deformed version of nominals of the form the fact + Sentence. Hence

(185) John's flying the plane disturbs me

is a reduced version of

(186) the fact that John flies the plane disturbs me[55]

The paraphrase relations among such pairs are obvious. But what syntactic justification can be offered for such a derivation? Observe that there is, in a sense, an 'intermediate form' of such nominals:

(187) the fact of John's flying the plane

This structure is a paraphrase of the earlier pair. Any English grammar must generate nominals like (187). But since the external distribution and internal co-occurrence relations of the (187) type are in essence identical with those of the (186) type, there is strong motivation for deriving the latter from the former. Interestingly enough, the rules required for this derivation are largely identical with those required to derive type (ii) nominals in (169) from the type (iv) nominals there. Thus we need rules which replace a form following a Noun by of and add the Genitive to the immediately following Noun Phrase; and a later rule which replaces present by -ing or NML in Genitive -----. We cannot say that the rules required in the case of fact are absolutely identical unless we make an assumption about whether or not the that + Sentence structure following fact is a relative phrase or not. On

this matter we take no position. If it is a relative structure, then
the rules needed are identical. If not, then some differences exist.
In either case, however, the derivations are closely enough related to require adding almost nothing to the syntactic component
to derive the analogues of (187) from those of (186), given our
earlier description of the formation of the types of nominal illustrated in (169).

However, according to the derivation of nominals like (187), the
simplest statement of the rule given earlier, $T_{gen\ sub}$, which derives type (i) nominals in (169) from type (ii) will automatically
derive

(188) *John's fact of flying the plane

This nonoccurring structure thus fills an otherwise empty position
in the derivations produced by $T_{gen\ sub}$. In other words, $T_{gen\ sub}$
is simpler if structures like (188) are generated. But exactly analogously to the derivation of John's driving of the car from *the
way of John's driving the car we can derive John's driving the car
from (188). Furthermore, essentially the same rule is needed in
both cases, namely a rule to replace a noun by an Auxiliary + Verb
that immediately follows of. The only difference is that where the
rule applies to the structure underlying (188), the noun fact rather
than way or manner is replaced, and the of is dropped instead of
retained as in the way case. This accounts for that superficial
contrast between the manner and factive constructions. This substitution of Auxiliary + Verb occurs, of course, only after the application of $T_{gen\ sub}$.

In short, John's driving the car fills an automatically generated
position in nominals derived from fact in the same way that John's
driving of the car fills a similar position in nominals derived
from way. Furthermore, the required reduction and deformation
rules are much the same in both cases, and they are basically the
same as the rules needed to describe a large class of distinct nominals based on nouns occurring as the heads of Adverbial constituents.

Our description of the factive construction accounts for the fact
that, unlike the manner construction, it may be based on any verbs
whatsoever, since there is no restriction other than to declaratives
on the verbal elements which can be the basis for the Sentence element in the fact that Sentence. It is not so clear, however, that
our description accounts for the failure of the factive construction
to contain adjectives, i.e., for the absence of

(189) *John's important driving the car

This syntactic deviance would follow automatically from the absence of

(190) *the important fact of John's driving the car

and this, in turn, from the absence of

(191) the important fact that John drives the car

However, (191) does not appear to be ungrammatical. But, as
Chomsky points out, the adjectives in examples of this type appear to be the only ones related to appositive rather than restric-
tive relative clauses. Hence, although (191) is grammatical, it
does not seem to have the kind of structure that would underlie
(190) through independently motivated rules. In any event, the
extent to which our description provides an explanation of the
presence or absense of adjectives in the two constructions will
remain an open question until the description of the 'factive' nominalizations is made far more precise.

We conclude that there is strong syntactic motivation for providing two distinct derivations for apparently identical nominals
of the form Noun Phrase + Genitive + Verb + ing. In the two derivations we have provided, these forms derive from verbs which
are either transitive with deletable object or intransitive. We
have seen that both forms are actually reduced versions of underlying nominals containing an occurrence of either fact or way.
Thus the resulting structurally ambiguous nominal form is ambiguous in just the way predicted by the contrasting meanings of
fact and way. As further support for this syntactic treatment, we
may point to cases where nominals of this type are not structurally
ambiguous, for example,

(192) John's driving is indubitable and uncontested

and

(193) John's driving is hurried and reckless

Example (192) bears only the factive interpretation, while (193)
bears only the manner interpretation. The support given by cases
such as these is appreciated when one realizes that the nonambiguity of each of these examples and their contrasting senses is
paralleled by restrictions on the distribution of the nouns fact and
way:

(194) a. the fact that John drives is indubitable and uncontested
       b. *the way that John drives is indubitable and uncontested

(195) a. *the fact that John drives is hurried and reckless
       b. the way that John drives is hurried and reckless

Thus we see that the nonambiguity of such nominals and of their
specific sense is predicted by our syntactic description on the
basis of the fact that only one of the two nominal sources is capable of occurring in a certain environment.

Therefore nominal constructions that are ambiguous between a
factive and a manner sense are not genuine counterexamples to

the general claim that the meaning of a sentence is determined by
the operation of projection rules upon underlying P-markers. As
we have argued, there are also syntactic grounds for claiming
that the underlying P-markers of these ambiguous nominals contain different elements, fact and way, which are exactly those required to account for the ambiguity involved, the specific sense
of each term of this ambiguity, and the cases where related nominals are not ambiguous. Furthermore, our syntactic treatment,
together with our general restriction of projection rules to operating on underlying P-markers, provides an extremely powerful
systematization of the paraphrase relations among the various related constructions involving factive nominals and among the various related constructions involving manner nominals.

Our final case of an apparent counterexample to the claim that
projection rules operate exclusively on underlying P-markers is
presented by certain examples of productive derivation. Consider,
for example,

(196) a. an employer of John's is foolish
       b. *the employer of John's is foolish
       c. that employer of John's is foolish
       d. John's employer is foolish

(197) a. an employee of John's is foolish
       b. *the employee of John's is foolish
       c. that employee of John's is foolish
       d. John's employee is foolish

The internal relations among these sets are fully accounted for by
differences in determiners. The d form can be considered to be
derived from the nonexistent b form by means of $T_{gen\ sub}$, which
was described earlier. Hence, the d forms are simply on a par
with the others, and the ungrammatical sequence has no deeper
significance than to serve as the origin for the d form.

It is evident that the sentences of (196) and (197) are, respectively, paraphrases of

(198) a. someone who employs John is foolish
       b. that one who employs John is foolish
       c. the one who employs John is foolish

(199) a. someone who John employs is foolish
       b. that one who John employs is foolish
       c. the one who John employs is foolish

Now consider the derivation of the structures in (196) and (197).
In the only previous generative treatment, those of (196) have been
derived transformationally by substituting a transformationally
altered version of the structure underlying someone employs John
for the Noun Phrase in a Matrix of the form Noun Phrase be foolish

This treatment requires a special generalized transformation for the generation of these agentive cases, a generalized transformation that substitutes the Auxiliary + Verb + Noun Phrase (with a preceding of added) for the Matrix Noun Phrase. This Auxiliary constituent is replaced by the agentive suffix, -er, which later shifts to the right of the verb by the usual rule for verb affixes. To make this treatment come out right, Lees required two preparatory singulary transformations (his T47 and T48) to produce the right forms of Constituent P-markers for the necessary generalized transformation.

The structures illustrated by (197) are obviously much less general in internal membership than that of (196), and we are not aware of any explicit generative treatment of them. If, however, they were treated in the same terms as the -ee case, the same general kind of Matrix and Constituent P-markers but a different special generalized transformation would be required. The latter would operate in much the same way as the former but would substitute -ee instead of -er for the Constituent P-marker Auxiliary and would be based on an equivalence of the Matrix Noun Phrase with the object Noun Phrase of the Constituent P-marker rather than with that of the subject Noun Phrase as in the -er case.

This kind of syntactical description of the -ee and -er derivatives, however, is incompatible with the theory of semantic interpretation developed previously, since, according to the description of these derivations in earlier paragraphs, sentences like

(200) I saw someone's employer

(201) I saw someone's employee

would have the same pair of underlying P-markers although they differ in meaning. These P-markers would be roughly those shown in Diagrams 4.21 and 4.22. In short, the treatment of derivational processes implied by Lees's grammatical treatment of agentives provides no way of accounting in our terms for the fact that, semantically, the derivatives in sentences like (196) refer to the

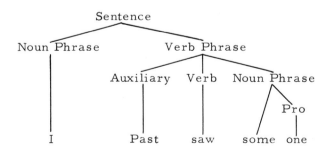

Diagram 4.21

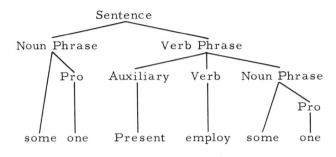

Diagram 4.22

subject of the P-marker containing employ while in (197) the derivatives refer to the object of that P-marker.

If our theory of semantic interpretation is to be preserved,
cases like these must be derived from distinct sets of underlying
P-markers, with these sets permitting a non-ad hoc derivation
of the correct semantic interpretations, particularly the correct
paraphrase relations between (196) and (197) and between (198)
and (199), respectively, and similarly in analogous cases. But
this result is easily achieved, since derivatives with -er and -ee
should clearly be derived, not by a special generalized transformation for each, but rather by a deforming singulary transformation
from the structures which underlie sentences like (198) and (199).
Verbal derivatives with -er and -ee must, in other words, be
looked at as slightly deformed versions of relative phrases. But
in the underlying structures of such phrases the subject-object
contrast is marked by the presence of an occurrence of wh in either
subject or object. We shall describe the required deformation
only briefly and only for the -er case, since the -ee derivation is
analogous.

The relative rule will automatically generate structures like
that shown in Diagram 4.23. We wish this structure to underlie
*the employer of John's, which in turn underlies the well-formed
John's employer. Clearly, one rule is required to replace the
Determiner dominating wh by of and to add the genitive formative
to the object Noun Phrase of the verb employ. This rule is very
similar to T_{of}, which operates for other nominalizations. These
rules can thus be combined to increase the generality of the description. A special rule is then needed to replace the Present
Tense morpheme by the agentive formative -er. Application of
these rules, plus the normal shift of the relative to the right of
the noun it modifies and deletion of the repeated noun, yields a
structure like that of Diagram 4.24.

At this point, another rule is required to substitute the Auxiliary + Verb for the Noun in front of the of. This rule is essentiall

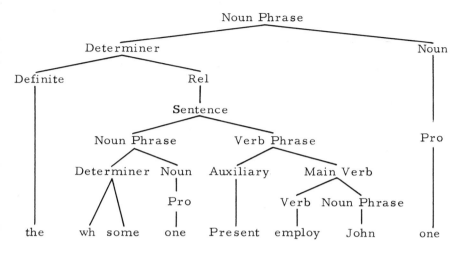

Diagram 4.23

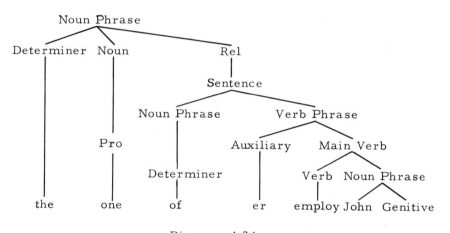

Diagram 4.24

identical with that required in our description of nominalizations
in -ing and NML. Thus, again, very little has to be added to the
grammar. It is, of course, necessary to restrict these rule applications in these cases to just those relative phrases which are
based on verbs having agentive forms.[57] Nonetheless, it is clear
that in terms of considerations of simplicity our description is
much to be preferred to that in which such derivatives are formed
by special generalized transformations. The present analysis,
with its analogue for the -ee case, accounts completely for the
restrictions on nominalized verbs of the -ee and -er types and
eliminates not only the special generalized transformation required by Lees (the extra pair of such rules required to extend

his treatment to the -ee case) but also his extra singulary transformations, namely T47 and T48. Furthermore, the derivation
from relatives that we have given accounts for some restrictions
that Lees was unable to handle. He noted that if his treatment
generated

(202) John is a miner

(203) John is the miner

it would also generate

(204) *a miner is John

But any English syntactic component must exclude

(205) *someone who mines is John

by an appropriate restriction on relatives and proper nouns. But
if agentive and objective verbal derivatives are obtained from relatives, as we suggest, the absence of sentences like (205) accounts
automatically for the fact that those like (204) are not well formed.

There is thus strong syntactic motivation for deriving verbal derivatives with -er and -ee suffixes from relative phrases which are
in turn, derived from Matrices with Rel constituents and appropria
Constituent P-markers. The only generalized transformation required is the realtive, which is needed independently. But under
this mode of derivation, the fact that (200) and (201) are different
in meaning, with the difference being one of subject versus object c
employ, is already accounted for purely in terms of the differences
between the underlying P-markers. In the Constituent P-marker
of the agentive case, wh will be attached to the subject Noun Phras
while in the objective case wh will be attached to the object Noun
Phrase. Hence, the apparatus introduced to handle questions and
relatives earlier also serves automatically to differentiate the underlying P-markers of contrasting derivatives in -ee and -er. To
obtain agentive and objective derivatives by deformation from relatives, which is the simplest syntactic treatment, automatically
accounts for the paraphrase relations between sets like (196) and
(198) and between (197) and (199), respectively, by showing that
all the corresponding pairs have identical sets of underlying P-
markers. Far from being counterexamples to our view of semanti
interpretation, the case of agentive and objective verbal derivative
is further strong support for this view.

NOTES

1. Chomsky (1957), pp. 100-101.

2. The syntactic motivation for this treatment comes partly from
its superiority in stating the co-occurrence relations between

passives and manner adverbials, and partly from its compatibility with a uniform formulation of the rules of derived
constituent structure. This treatment also permits a generalization of the structure index of the passive transformation
to mention the constituent Verb rather than $Verb_{transitive}$
and hence provides an automatic account of pseudo passives
based on verbs of type other than transitive, such as the bed
was slept in by Harry.

3. We are indebted to N. Chomsky for this argument.

4. Lees (1960), p. 19; Klima (1964).

5. For a discussion of the reading of Negative and the way negative sentences are interpreted, cf. Katz (1964 b).

6. Actually the meaning appears to be what is common to the
readings of this list of verbs.

7. We assume that (37), (38) and all following examples have
the intonation of single sentences.

8. Lees (1960), pp. 5-6.

9. On the basis of (41)-(44) plus the fact that there are no sentences like *I request that you want to go, *I request that you
hope to be famous, a case can be made for deriving imperatives syntactically from sentences of the form I $Verb_{request}$
that you will Main Verb by dropping at least the first three
elements. This would account not only for (41)-(44) but also
for the facts represented in (35)-(40). Such a derivation
would permit dispensing with I and its reading RIM and would
simplify the semantic component by eliminating one entry. It
would also eliminate from the syntax all the necessary heavy
selectional restrictions on I and the rules that must introduce
this element. Although we do not adopt this description here,
it certainly deserves further study. Either the derivation with
I or the one just suggested supports our main point that the
underlying P-markers of imperatives are different from those
of declaratives in the semantically relevant ways.

10. Chomsky (1957, 1962); Lees (1960). An exception to this is
the treatment of Klima (1962), in which a single wh morpheme
was postulated at the beginning of underlying P-markers. This
element was then the mark of questions and provided an environment which made the auxiliary inversion question transformation obligatory rather than optional. It will be evident
that this treatment of Klima's is much closer to that which we
suggest here than the earlier one, represented, say, by
Chomsky's (1957) description, although it still does not meet
the conditions we require. Cf. our discussion on pp. 110-111.

11. Cf. Chomsky (1964 b) for a discussion of this syntactic mo-
    tivation for the principle of unique recoverability as well as
    other arguments for this principle with respect to the syn-
    tactic structure of English, especially the behavior of ques-
    tion and relative forms.

12. Chomsky (1964 b).

13. Free deletability is characterized by the constraint just be-
    low.

14. Until recently there was difficulty in actually formalizing this
    notion of 'necessarily identical'. This would present no prob-
    lem if the transformation which does the deleting or substituting
    itself always contained a condition guaranteeing that the ith
    term is identical to some other term. But there appear to be
    cases of substitution and deletion transformations which must
    delete strings whose identity to other strings is guaranteed,
    not by their own equivalence condition, but by the equivalence
    conditions of some previously applied transformation. A sug-
    gestion of Chomsky, too recent to be incorporated in the text,
    has eliminated this problem, however, and contributed greatly
    to the simplification of grammars. He has proposed, in cases
    where some string s_i of $s_1 \ldots s_n$ is to be deleted subject to
    identity to some other string in $s_1 \ldots s_n$, that s_i be substituted
    for this other string. The general theory will then ensure
    that a non-pro-form can only be substituted for if the string
    being substituted is strongly identical to that which it replaces.
    'Strongly identical' here means identical not only terminally
    but in its higher constituent structure. This solves the prob-
    lem of 'necessary identity' and permits the elimination of the
    identity conditions from the grammars of particular languages.
    Thus, for example, in the derivation of relative phrases like
    the man that came from the structure schematically indicated
    by the + man + wh + a + man came, the second instance of
    man is substituted for the first. And there is no need for the
    rule which accomplishes this to mention identity, since if the
    nouns are not identical, the condition of the general theory of
    the syntactic component guarantees that the operation cannot
    occur. This suggestion of Chomsky's thus builds the notion
    of 'necessarily identical' into the general theory of linguistic
    descriptions in a precise and very strong way.

15. There is a rule attaching articles to following nouns that are
    instances of Pro, subject to many restrictions. Thus the out-
    put forms are single words, something, it, there, etc. The
    relevant rule is discussed in greater detail but still informally
    in Section 4.3.

16. We mean of course 'hears in isolation', i.e., without any in-
    formation supplied by context. Throughout this work we are

interested in specifying the contribution which the linguistic
system alone makes to the understanding of sentences.

17. The marker that replaces (Selector) by the stated equivalence must be considered a <u>compound marker.</u> Cf. Katz
(1964 b).

18. Besides (Selector), the dictionary entries for pro-forms contain ordinary semantic markers like (Human), (Male), etc.
There is evidently a universal restriction on the set of such
markers that can be assigned to pro-forms; i.e., these are
restricted to a few of the most general markers found in the
readings of the lexical items of the category to which a particular pro-form belongs. We do not yet know how to build
this restriction into the general theory of linguistic descriptions. We recognize that this fact plus an uncertainty as to
how the constituent Pro is to be generated lends a good deal
of vagueness to the description of pro-forms just given.

19. Of course, some imperatives are concerned with eliciting
linguistic responses, as are, <u>say cheese,</u> <u>tell me your name,</u>
etc. However, the linguistic aspect of such imperatives is
clearly a function of the nonimperative elements they contain
and presents no special problems. Similarly, some answers
are nonlinguistic, as are shrugs, gestures, pointing, groans,
etc. But the latter may be considered derivative for verbal
answers. Thus we claim that nonlinguistic answers have
roughly the same status as writing with respect to the spoken
language.

20. English has devices for permitting less clumsy paraphrases
of (73): <u>I request that you answer whether or not you will go</u>
<u>home, I request that you answer if you will go home or not,</u>
<u>I request that you answer if you will or will not go home.</u>
These may be transformationally related to the structures
underlying (73).

21. A somewhat later though unpublished treatment of these
questions (Klima, 1964) postulated the introduction of a
single <u>wh</u> morpheme in the front of underlying P-markers.
Our discussion will in fact use this as a basis for criticism
since all criticisms of this position carry over to the earlier
and published descriptions. Cf. Chomsky (1957) and Lees
(1960).

22. The relations between elements like (81)c, d, and (82) have
been studied extensively by Klima (in preparation). It seems
that they can be generally characterized by positing the introduction of a special formative, X, in certain contexts which
include Negative and Q, <u>some + X</u> = <u>any, anytimes</u> = <u>ever,</u>
etc. In some cases the introduction of X is optional. Hence,

alongside (82)d one finds: does he eat $\left\{ \begin{array}{l} \text{some meat} \\ \text{somewhere} \end{array} \right\}$. That is, in some question contexts the forms with or without X may be found, but in otherwise identical contexts only the forms without X. Thus the ungrammatical (82)c corresponds to: he eats $\left\{ \begin{array}{l} \text{some meat} \\ \text{somewhere} \end{array} \right\}$.

23. In these cases of ungrammatical elements, and certain others cited below, as Example (109), it is necessary to assume one is considering nonecho forms. If these utterances are considered to have rising (incredulity) intonation on the wh-form, they are perhaps regarded as grammatical echoes. Later we suggest that echo questions are related to emphasis, but it is not known how emphasis relates to the possibility of co-occurrence with otherwise prohibited elements in questions.

24. For a discussion of semisentences, cf. Chomsky (1964 a) and Katz (1964 a).

25. The process for producing semisentences of this type is presumably a universal. It is to be sharply distinguished from language particular processes of providing answers like Booth did, which is an appropriate answer to (89) and in context is a paraphrase of (90), being in a sense a 'pro-version' of the latter. In other words, we claim that English grammar contains specific rules that derive the sentence Booth did but none that derives utterances like (93) and (94). The understandability of the latter must be explained in terms of the ability of speakers to use context to recover full sentences from fragmentary representatives thereof.

26. This is not the strongest argument for deriving these single-word question forms from unspecified indefinites of the form some X. For stronger arguments, cf. Chomsky (1964 b) and Postal (in preparation a).

27. For extensive discussion of this and other points relating to questions, cf. Postal (in preparation a).

28. We suspect that other semantic properties besides questioning require universal scope markers like wh — for example, negation or emphasis. For a discussion of the case of negation, cf. Katz (1964 b).

29. We thus disagree with the position taken by Weinreich that there might be languages in which prepositions and similar elements are questioned. Cf. Weinreich (1963).

30. Fillmore (1962).

31.   We are indebted to Miss Jacqueline Wei for this observation.
      This fact about need for conjunction adds some weight to the
      suggestion that sequences of adverbs, even of different types,
      be generated by conjunction transformations, with each un-
      derlying P-marker restricted to the occurrence of one such
      Adverb. Cf. Stockwell (1960).

32.   Cf. Chomsky (1957) p. 112. In this rule, subscripted brack-
      ets with identical numbers indicate that the compressed ex-
      pressions may be expanded out only line by line. Hence, when
      the fourth term is Tense plus null, the fifth must be Verb plus
      Y; when the fourth is Tense plus have, be or Modal, the fifth
      must be Y.

33.   This feature of questions was first brought to light and form-
      alized by Chomsky [(1957), p. 67]. The resulting analysis al-
      so provides the basis for treatment of related forms with got.
      The rules for introduction of got (which is sometimes obliga-
      tory) are largely given in Chomsky (1962).

34.   This fact about Rule (T2) raises important technical questions
      about transformational grammars. First, each transforma-
      tion must have a unique output when applied to a particular
      P-marker so that technically Rule (T2) is not a transformation
      but a family of transformations. In fact, it is perhaps best to
      view all of the rules of actual grammars as families, many
      perhaps containing only a single member. A family of trans-
      formations is a set (perhaps even infinite in number) finitely
      characterized by a fixed condition on structure indices. Sec-
      ond, in order for a P-marker containing have as a Verb to be
      ambiguously analyzable in terms of Rule (T2), it is necessary
      to permit the use of null elements in bracketing P-markers
      for transformational application. This presents no real dif-
      ficulty since in the concatenation algebra underlying formal
      linguistics any string of the form a + b + c + ... + n is equiv-
      alent to a concatenation of the form a + null + b + null + c +
      null + ... + null + n. Hence, all the required null elements
      are provided in a non-ad hoc way by the underlying concatena-
      tion algebra. The nulls provide a nonunique bracketing for
      strings in the case of Rule (T2) because the structure index
      of this rule itself mentions a null.

35.   This analysis appears to provide a simpler and more adequate
      treatment of the intonational facts about questions, even in its
      present form, than does Chomsky's [(1957) p. 71] briefly and
      hesitantly suggested explanation.

36.   It was not noted before that there is a single universal P1 that
      applies in all cases of unary branchings, i.e., those of the form

$$A$$
$$\uparrow$$
$$B$$

(B terminal or not), to associate trivially the set of readings
of B with A.

37. Actually we ignore here an intermediate constituent, called
Theme, which, with an optional preceding Sentence Adverbial
constituent, is dominated by Nucleus. Thus it is Theme which,
we claim, is developed into Noun Phrase + Verb Phrase.

38. Cf. Collingwood (1946) and Strawson (1956) for the philosophical background for this notion, and also its importance in the
discussion of certain outstanding philosophical problems.

39. The definition of entailment in terms of a semantic theory of
a natural language is given in Katz (1964 b).

40. G. H. Matthews, personal communication.

41. This treatment of intuitive relations among sentence types
in no way assimilates transformational descriptions to phrase
structure descriptions by replacing transformations by extra
constituents in phrase structure grammars, as suggested by
Hockett (1961). Hockett's suggestion amounts, of course, to
discarding the possibility of associating sets of P-markers
with sentences and reduces the SD of each sentence to a
single P-marker. The inadequacies of this treatment have
been discussed earlier. Cf. also Postal (1964). Furthermore, Hockett's suggestion is simply impossible for generalized transformations.

   In a phrase structure grammar such universal elements as
Q and wh could be posited but not justified. That is, in such
restricted terms it would be impossible to show, for example,
that both yes-no and wh-questions contain both Q and wh, etc.
Hence, the shift in the way transformational grammars explicate intuitive relations among sentences related by singulary transformations, which we propose, does not amount to
accepting the limitations of phrase structure description for
these phenomena, and the proposed explanation is not in fact
justifiable in exclusively phrase structure terms. Universal
elements like Q, I, etc., make sense only if posited in underlying P-markers.

42. Chomsky (1957), pp. 88-91.

43. We are basing our interpretation on Chomsky's explicit statement "Further transformational analysis would show that in
both cases the sentence is a transform of the pair of terminal
strings that underlie the simple kernel sentences: (110)(i) I
found the boy, and (ii) the boy is studying in the library. Hence,

this is an interesting case of a sentence whose ambiguity is the result of alternative transformational developments from the same kernel strings." Cf. Chomsky (1957), p. 88. But in his actual transformational analysis of this case, Chomsky gives a description which is inconsistent with the previously quoted statement and which is almost the same as the description we have given above. Cf. Chomsky (1957), pp. 76-79, especially rule (91).

44. This has been suggested, in effect, for English quite independently of the present work. Cf. Chomsky (1962) and Fillmore (1963).

45. Chomsky (1964 b).

46. For a discussion, cf. Lees (1960). Although we have profited from his discussion, our analysis below is incompatible with his. We also disagree with some of his factual observations.

47. Lees (1960), p. 68.

48. The irregularity of NML led Lees to certain apparently erroneous conclusions about the second construction that we are considering. Thus he claimed [(1960), p. 66] that 'non-action' verbs do not form such nominals as those in (160), and to support this he offered the impossible forms *his believing of it and *his admiring of her, but note his belief of it and his admiration of her. Which verbs are found in these nominals appears to be determined by co-occurrence with manner adverbials, and nothing else.

49. Lees (1960) and Chomsky (1964 b).

50. This structure is, of course, well formed on a genitive derivation, but this is irrelevant to the present discussion.

51. In personal conversation.

52. There is some possibility that -ing and NML may be identified. These elements are, of course, introduced in several other constructions.

53. Cf. our discussion in the next paragraph, which shows that the structure of this impossible form underlies an actually occurring sequence and hence must be generated.

54. This description of the genitive is based on unpublished work by Chomsky.

55. Actually, there is some reason to doubt that the reduction is from strings containing fact. It is more likely, as suggested by Chomsky (personal communication), that the Noun which is deleted is the pro-form of the Noun subcategory to which

fact and many other similar nouns, like idea, reason, etc.,
belong. This pro-form is probably it, which is dropped in
front of that + S sequences and which is also more semantically unspecific than fact. The presence of an unspecified
element like it is suggested by such sentences as John's
flying the plane is doubtful, which is hardly a paraphrase of
the contradictory sentence the fact that John flies the plane
is doubtful. A revision of our analysis along these lines
would not really affect our fundamental argument, since what
we have been calling the 'factive' sense of nominalizations is
actually less specific than this term suggests.

56. Lees (1960), pp. 70-71.

57. The verbs having agentive versions are mainly those which
have passives, i.e., which take manner adverbials. Thus it
is possible that those relatives which are actually deformed
into agentive nominals are only those which can undergo the
passive transformation. This would explain the exclusion of
verbs with complements (intend, hope, want), middle verbs,
have, etc.

Chapter 5

CONCLUSION

5.1 A Heuristic Principle

Throughout the discussion of apparent counterexamples we have tacitly made use of a principle whose explicit formulation should have heuristic value for those engaged in investigating syntactic structure. This principle, it should be stressed, is not a statement in the linguistic description of a language, nor is it a statement in linguistic theory, but rather it is a rule of thumb based on the general character of linguistic descriptions. The principle can be stated as follows: Given a sentence for which a syntactic derivation is needed; look for simple paraphrases of the sentence which are not paraphrases by virtue of synonymous expressions; on finding them, construct grammatical rules that relate the original sentence and its paraphrases in such a way that each of these sentences has the same sequence of underlying P-markers. Of course, having constructed such rules, it is still necessary to find independent syntactic justification for them.

A remark should be added here about the requirement in this heuristic principle that the paraphrases of the given sentence not be paraphrases by virtue of synonymous expressions. Although any two sentences that are transformationally related through having the same set of underlying P-markers are ipso facto paraphrases of each other, the converse is not the case. Sentences that are not so related can be paraphrases of each other on the basis of containing expressions that are synonymous.[1]

5.2 Implications for the Syntactic Component

In Chapter 4 we considered some analyses of the syntax of English sentences and suggested several revisions and extensions of previous treatments. Furthermore, certain of the comments made there had implications for the general theory of syntax. These included postulation of the restriction of embeddings to replacing specified dummy elements, postulation of Rel and Comp with md representatives, suggestion of universality of Q, I, wh, Negative, Passive, and the suggestion of a universal set of conditions introducing question-relevant wh in the underlying P-markers of all languages. Our earlier discussions showed that adequate linguistic descriptions require

157

a very rich theory of syntax, one rich enough to characterize at
least such notions as modifier, Noun Phrase, a constituent that
can be 'questioned', and a sentence-type marker. In the present
section we shall consider some further implications for the character of the syntactic component that may be derived from the fact
that a linguistic description must contain a semantic component of
the form described in this monograph.

First, the arguments given to show that projection rules must
operate exclusively on underlying P-markers provide in themselves sufficient motivation for having a transformational syntactic component. Virtually every argument given in the past to establish the empirical adequacy of the SD provided by transformational grammars, as against those of exclusively phrase structure
grammars,[2] has a formal analogue from semantic theory to establish the same point of relative adequacy. Each analogue has
the form of an argument showing that any adequate semantic component must operate on the underlying P-markers of sentences,
but not on any of their derived P-markers. Equivalents of the
derived P-markers enumerated by transformational syntactic components (in fact, equivalents of the final derived P-markers) are,
in effect, the only aspect of syntactic structure which can, in
principle, be countenanced by exclusively phrase-structure conceptions of the syntactic component. Hence, if adequate linguistic
descriptions require reference to underlying P-markers to provide
correct semantic interpretations for sentences, then exclusively
phrase-structure syntactic components and the theory of language
which requires them are inadequate. The only available alternatives to the transformational conception of the syntactic component are versions of the theory of phrase-structure grammar
in the precise sense of Chomsky.[3] Therefore, showing that adequate linguistic descriptions require reference to underlying P-
markers is sufficient to justify the transformational conception
of the syntactic component.

Second, there is a major implication from these syntactic considerations, namely that there exists a partially universal characterization of the structure of underlying P-markers. Of course,
this structure cannot be completely universal. For example, un-
questionably there are languages without a separate major constituent of adjectives (e.g., Iroquoian), and this difference from
Indo-European languages and others is obvious. Nonetheless,
there is sufficient similarity between the underlying P-markers
of different languages to suggest many universal features. There
appears to be always a Noun Phrase which is subject; in other
cases there are both a Noun Phrase subject and Noun Phrase object; there is a single element whose morpheme membership
is strongly determined by subject Noun Phrase and object Noun
Phrase (if there is one), which is the constituent Verb; there is

the optional presence of various kinds of adverbial elements (always the same ones), sentence adverbials of time, place, manner, condition, quantity, purpose, etc.   The striking fact is that the semantic relations between these elements appear to be the same in different languages.   That is, the projection rules needed to combine the markers of subject Noun Phrase and Verb in English are identical with those needed for this combination in French, Mohawk, etc., and similarly for combinations of the other elements just mentioned.   Consequently, unless such notions as 'subject Noun Phrase' and 'Verb' are characterized in the general theory of the syntactic component, essentially identical projection rules will have to be included ad hoc in the semantic components of all languages.   The natural suggestion is, therefore, that all the notions required for a universal statement of the constituents and relations involved in these universal projection rules be characterized in the general theory.   This task involves a universal characterization not only of major constituents like Noun Phrase, Verb, Adverb$_x$, etc., but also of the basic relations.   But since the basic grammatical relations appear to be definable in terms of constituent configurations in underlying P-markers, a universal characterization of such relations requires a universal set of major constituent configurations.   For example, if in English the subject relation is definable in terms of the configuration (Sentence: Noun Phrase, Verb Phrase), and if this characterization is to be made universal by the configuration technique discussed earlier, then the subject Noun Phrase must always precede the Verb in the underlying P-markers of all languages.   The very real differences of major constituent order found in the actual sentences of natural languages must then be due to transformational operations.   This universality of underlying P-marker structure must of course be implemented by providing universal rules that partially characterize underlying phrase markers.   We have already suggested some such rules, namely those which introduce md representatives of Rel and Comp, those which introduce wh, and those which introduce sentence-type markers such as Q, I, Negative, Passive (to which should, no doubt, be added Emphasis, Exclamation, and perhaps others).   Thus we see that these rules must in all likelihood be extended to include the introduction rules for at least the major constituents.

5.3 Universals in Linguistic Descriptions

This monograph has been concerned with formulating a theory of linguistic descriptions.   In this section, we shall describe in abstract terms our conception of the kind of theory we have been formulating.   In particular, we wish to describe how a theory of linguistic descriptions systematizes statements expressing linguistic universals.

To characterize the notion 'linguistic description of a natural language' it is necessary to distinguish two aspects of such descriptions: that part which concerns features of the language which make it different from other languages and that part which concerns features common to all natural languages. In short, one must distinguish those features of a language that it has by virtue of being English, French, Chinese, etc., as opposed to one of the others, from those features it has by virtue of being a natural language. A full specification of the latter set of features is a theory of the structure of natural language, and the features specified are the universals of language.

Universals of language are of two different types: <u>substantive universals</u> and <u>formal universals</u>. A linguistic description is a theory and, as such, consists of a set of statements formulated in a fixed theoretical vocabulary. The distinction between substantive and formal universals is intended to correspond to the distinction between the form of such statements and their content. Thus a formal universal is a specification of the form of a statement in a linguistic description, while a substantive universal is a concept or set of concepts out of which particular statements in a linguistic description are constructed. The list of all substantive universals that the theory of linguistic descriptions makes available to particular linguistic descriptions is the stock of theoretical concepts that may be drawn upon in the construction of the rules and lexical formulations of a given linguistic description. On the other hand, the list of all formal universals presents the alternative ways in which a given linguistic description can formulate a generalization about the language it describes.

Examples of substantive universals are: the phonological concepts of vocality, compactness, phoneme; the syntactic concepts of Noun Phrase, modifier, Q, <u>wh</u>; and the semantic concepts of (Male), (Physical Object), (Process), (Selector). These are the theoretical concepts in terms of which descriptive rules of the phonological, syntactic, and semantic components are formulated. Examples of formal universals can be more or less detailed. An example of one of the most detailed formal universals is a specification that certain rules must be found in the syntactic component of any linguistic description — for example, the rule Rel → md. An example of one of the least detailed formal universals is the specification that some of the rules of a syntactic component be transformational in form.

Besides these two types of universals, the theory of linguistic descriptions contains a specification of the form of each of the three components of a linguistic description, i.e., a specification of the interrelations between the members of a set of rules which give that set its systematic character. Examples of such

specifications are the ordering of phonological rules and the restriction that in a syntactic derivation singulary transformations
do not apply to a P-marker which has been embedded in another
P-marker.[4] Such specifications for the phonological, syntatic,
and semantic components, together with the statement of the substantive and formal universals for those components, provide a
characterization of the notions 'syntactic component', 'phonological component', and 'semantic component'.

Finally, a theory of linguistic descriptions contains a specification of the interconnections between the three components of
any particular linguistic description. This provides the final step
in characterizing the notion 'linguistic description of a natural
language'. In this monograph we have proposed the specification
of these interrelations that is pictured in Diagram 5.1.

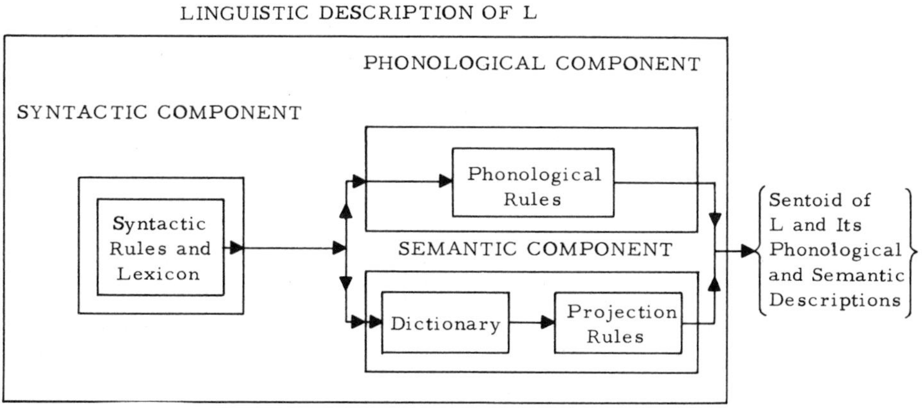

LINGUISTIC DESCRIPTION OF L

Diagram 5.1

We noted at the beginning of this study that a tripartite theory
of linguistic descriptions can explain the Saussurian dictum that
the relation between form and meaning is arbitrary. In terms
of the more precise conception of linguistic description developed
in the intervening pages, we can substantiate and deepen this
claim. The semantic component, as we have seen, operates exclusively on the underlying P-markers of sentences, i.e., on the
most abstract aspect of syntactic structure. The phonological
component, however, operates on the final derived P-markers
of sentences,[5] the most superficial aspect of syntactic structure.
These components operate independently of each other because
they operate on quite distinct aspects of the output of the syntactic
component and because neither takes into account the operations
of the other in determining any phase of its own operation. Therefore, there is necessarily a resultant lack of correlation between
the outputs of the two interpretative components, and this lack of

correlation between phonetic and semantic properties explains
Saussure's dictum.

We may clarify the idea of a formal universal if we consider
in more detail some further examples. Turning our attention
first to the syntactic component, we find that some of the rules
that will appear in this component will be fully determined by the
theory of linguistic descriptions, but that most will only be partially specified by this theory. Rules such as Comp → md, rules
that introduce major constituents, rules that introduce Q, etc.,
will be fully specified. Outside of the rules which generate underlying P-markers, there may be fully specified rules that determine the placement of word boundaries, and possibly universal rules that produce alternative orders of major constituents
under certain conditions.

In the case of the phonological component, again we find that
the presence of some rules is fully determined by the theory of
linguistic descriptions (a larger group, we think, than has previously been recognized), but that the presence of most rules is
due to idiosyncratic features of the language. Nevertheless,
certain aspects of the <u>form</u> of these rules are specified by the
theory of linguistic descriptions. Of the former kind are rules
such as

$$\begin{bmatrix} + \text{ Sonorant} \\ -\text{Consonantal} \end{bmatrix} \rightarrow \begin{bmatrix} + \text{ Vocalic} \end{bmatrix} \text{ and } \begin{bmatrix} + \text{ Vocalic} \\ - \text{ Consonantal} \end{bmatrix} \rightarrow \begin{bmatrix} + \text{ Sonorant} \end{bmatrix},$$

for it appears that every language has two primary classificatory
distinctive features. One of them is always Consonantal, while
the other is either Sonorant or Vocalic. Whichever of these two
is chosen, the other is redundant and is specified <u>for vowels</u> by
one or the other of these two universal morpheme structure
rules.[6] Other universal phonological rules include those which
assert that the morpheme boundary is always phonetically null
and that the word boundary is either phonetically null or phonetically a pause. There appear to be many other universal rules
that account for the restrictions on combinations of classificatory
and phonetic distinctive features found in all languages. On the
other hand, a phonological rule that is characteristic of English
alone is the one which says that tense stops are aspirated in initial position. Linguistic theory does not specify that such a statement must occur in every phonological component (which would,
for example, be incompatible with the phonetic facts of French
or Spanish). It merely insists that if such a statement occurs, it
must have such and such a form.

In regard to the semantic component, the set of projection rules
is the same for all languages, i.e., is fully determined by the general theory of linguistic descriptions because differences between
Pl's depend on differences between grammatical relations, and

all languages draw their stock of grammatical relations from the same universal set. On the other hand, the dictionary of the semantic component, although formulated by using substantive and formal universals, is obviously determined in part by idiosyncratic features of individual languages. Semantic differences between languages are then wholly attributable to differences between the entries in the dictionaries of these languages and to differences in their underlying P-markers.

It was possible to give a universal characterization of the P2 because the only syntactic concepts required by this rule are themselves directly characterized in the general theory of linguistic descriptions, i.e., the notions of T-markers, matrix dummies, etc. A cross-linguistic general characterization of Pl requires similarly that all the syntactic notions mentioned in Pl be universally defined. However, the range of syntactic notions utilized in the formulation of Pl is far richer than that found in the P2.

Pl operate differently on different configurations in underlying P-markers. In other words, Pl apply to an underlying P-marker on the basis of the grammatical relations which hold between its elements. One distinct Pl is needed for each different grammatical relation. For example, in a configuration of the form shown in Diagram 5.2, the readings of B and C are amalgamated differently if B is the Main Verb and C the object Noun Phrase than if B is an adverbial modifier and C the Verb. In the latter case, a reading of the modifier is adjoined in a specified manner to a reading of the head, while in the former case, a reading of the object Noun Phrase is embedded at a fixed place in a reading of the Verb. However, even if a specific kind of syntactic relation holds between B and C — e.g., the modifier-head relation — amalgamation will occur in one way if B is the head and in another way if C is the head.

Diagram 5.2

Thus the syntactic information that the Pl require to do their work in the most economical manner includes a characterization of the full set of grammatical relations holding between elements in underlying P-markers. We have seen that particular individual grammatical relations can be defined in terms of subconfigurations of constituents. However, the kinds of notions required by Pl include more general concepts than individual grammatical relations, and include those which cover whole sets of such configurationally defined relations. That is, the syntactic facts represented by configurations of particular labeled bracketings are too low-level to permit an economical statement of the projection rules in the semantic component.

For example, in underlying P-markers one will find the elements shown in Diagrams 5.3-5.5. Even with a configurational

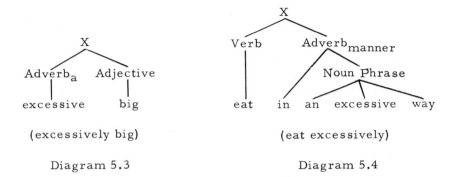

(excessively big)   (eat excessively)

Diagram 5.3   Diagram 5.4

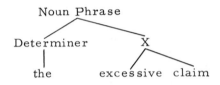

(the excessive claim)

Diagram 5.5

account of the relations which hold between the pairs of elements
in these structures, the semantic component would have to mul-
tiply the number of P1 by having a separate rule for each case
because there are different configurations dominated by each of
the constituents labeled 'X' and different directions of modification. Yet the semantic process of amalgamation is the same for
each pair of readings which must be assigned to a node labeled
'X' in these diagrams, and any adequate semantic component must
represent this fact in a formal way by having a single P1 for all
such cases. Thus the syntactic component of English must somehow show that all of the

configurations in Diagrams 5.3-5.5 have the formal property of
modification and must indicate the direction in each case.[7]
    However, the arguments just given show that it is not enough
for the syntactic component of English to characterize such notions as 'subject' and 'modifier'. This characterization must be
accomplished within the general theory of linguistic descriptions,
for besides the underlying configurations of Diagrams 5.3-5.5,
we shall certainly find, for example, such parallel elements in
Spanish, as shown in Diagrams 5.6-5.8. But now the semantic

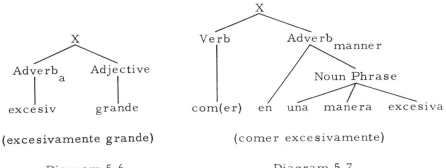

(excesivamente grande)

Diagram 5.6

(comer excesivamente)

Diagram 5.7

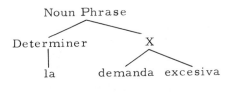

Diagram 5.8

relations and required amalgamations for readings are obviously
identical in the corresponding pairs of Diagrams 5.3-5.5 and
5.6-5.8. The assignment of readings to the nodes labeled 'X' is
formally the same in the two sets. Hence, the same considerations of simplicity and empirical adequacy which show that the
similarity between Diagrams 5.3-5.5 must be represented by the
syntactic component of English also show that the similarities
between the two sets of P-markers must be represented in the
general theory of linguistic descriptions. There must be a single
P1, specified in the general theory of linguistic descriptions, for
each distinct grammatical relation found in natural language. Thus
the same P1 will handle amalgamations of the readings for configurationally distinct instances of the same grammatical relation
in both the same and different languages, while different P1 will
deal with cases of different grammatical relations in the same
and different languages. Consequently, the syntactic information
required to characterize the appropriate grammatical relations
needed by these P1 must be provided uniformly by the syntactic
component of each linguistic description. The optimal way of
providing this syntactic information is to define the requisite
grammatical relations in the theory of linguistic descriptions.
   Since the configurational account of grammatical relations requires reference to such constituents as Noun Phrase, Verb
Phrase, and Adjective, these constituents must themselves be
given a universal characterization in the theory of linguistic

descriptions. This is the basis for the conclusion, reached in
our discussion of substantive universals, that a significant portion of the structure of underlying P-markers must be universally characterizable.

In short, a reasonable conception of the semantic component
imposes a minimal condition of adequacy upon the theory of the
syntactic component. This condition includes the fundamental
aim of traditional universal grammar, namely that a theory of
the syntactic component provide a cross-linguistic characterization not only of the form of syntactic rules and their interrelations but also of a significant portion of the content of such rules.
The aim of traditional universal grammar was in effect to provide
the concepts or categories in terms of which linguistic rules could
be stated. Interest in the goal of specifying the form of linguistic
rules is recent and is due to the influence of Chomsky. As we
have seen, the construction of the syntactic component in accord
with the theory of transformational syntax makes the achievement
of the traditional goal a real possibility by permitting the restriction of such cross-linguistic characterizations to the properties
of such highly abstract objects as underlying P-markers.

5.4 Implications for Models of Speech Recognition and Speech Production

A full linguistic description of a language would specify all the
knowledge of linguistic structure that enables a speaker to produce
and understand any sentence. But it would not describe how the
speaker actually uses this knowledge in producing and understanding
sentences. Thus a linguistic description represents linguistic
structure in the same sense in which an axiomatic mathematical
system represents the true statements about the domain of the
system. In both cases, the rules of the system simply define the
notion 'derivation within the system'. The rules of a linguistic
description no more describe how the speaker produces or understands sentences than the rules of a mathematical system describe the way in which proofs are written out or checked.

The syntactic component, which is the generative source for
the whole linguistic description, enumerates the infinite set of
sentoids in an order and in a way that must be considered essentially random from the viewpoint of actual speech production
and comprehension. The phonological and semantic components
cannot change this fact, because they are merely interpretative
devices which assign interpretations to sentoids in whatever order
those sentoids are given to them by the syntactic component.
Therefore, within the framework of a linguistic description, there
is no provision for describing how speakers equipped with a linguistic description of their language can extract from it just the
sentences they wish to produce and just the analyses required to

understand the sentences produced by others. The systematic
description of these abilities is the province of what can be called
'models of speech production' and 'models of speech recognition'.

Investigation of the problem of formulating a model of speech
recognition has developed partly from a concern with a somewhat
different problem,[8] namely that of providing a decision procedure
for syntactic well-formedness with respect to an arbitrary syntactic component. This is the question of whether, given a syntactic component C, there is a mechanical procedure definable
in terms of C which permits one to decide, for any given string
S in the terminal vocabulary of C, if S is derivable by the rules
of C and, if so, what syntactic description C assigns to S. It
was found, on the basis of empirically plausible assumptions
about the formal properties of transformational rules (in particular imposing a constraint equivalent to the restriction on deletions and substitutions mentioned in Chapter 4) that such a procedure could be given. However, even if these assumptions are
correct and the set of strings generated by a syntactic component
is recursive, the procedures cannot be regarded as acceptable
models of the way a human speaker obtains the syntactic structure of utterances. Such procedures fail as models of speech
recognition because of their extremely uneconomical character.
That is, the number of independent operations required by such
procedures to provide the syntactic analysis of even a twenty-
word sentence is so astronomically high that a human brain
could not conceivably obtain the syntactic structure even in a life-
time if it had to perform these operations. Hence, although these
procedures show how the linguistic information which a linguistic
description contains can be extracted to characterize the syntactic structure of a presented utterance, and although the ability to
do this must underlie the speaker's ability to understand sentences,
the specific means that such procedures utilize for extracting this
linguistic information cannot be the means that the speaker himself actually uses when he essentially instantaneously understands
the sentences he hears.

Thus, in order to convert a decision procedure into a model of
speech recognition, it is necessary to add a set of heuristics, i.e.,
schemes for radically cutting down the number of operations required by the procedure to assign a given sentence the syntactic
description it receives from the syntactic component. The over-
all system consisting of the decision procedure modified by a set
of such heuristics has been referred to as 'analysis by synthesis'.
Such a system recognizes an input sentence by applying the rules
of the syntactic component C in such a way that every derivable
string in the terminal vocabulary of C equal in length to a given
input string α is generated and assigned to a special set ω. Then
α is compared with each member of ω until an exact match is

found. When this happens, the system assigns to α the syntactic
analysis of the member of ω that matches α. There are also ef-
fective techniques for assigning n distinct syntactic structures
to α in case it is n-ways syntactically ambiguous. But we shall
ignore this refinement here. The heuristics serve to cut down
the size of ω and to reduce the steps required to generate ω.
Before the addition of such heuristics, the recognition procedure
takes advantage of essentially only one property of a string of
formatives that it receives, namely its length. The heuristics
are thus significant additions because they capitalize on syntactic
and phonetic properties of input strings which go beyond mere
length.

It is just at this point that the results of this monograph bear
on the problem of formulating a model of speech recognition.
These results deal with two questions that have to be answered
in formulating a model of speech recognition. First, what syntactic properties of input strings can be utilized by such a model
and how are they utilized? Second, what sort of syntactic description must be assigned to an input sentence by such a model?

Let us answer the second question first. The understanding of
a sentence, according to the conception of a linguistic description developed in the preceding pages, is obtaining its semantic
interpretation. According to this conception of how a speaker
understands a sentence, all that a model of speech recognition
is required to assign as a syntactic description to an input sentence to obtain its semantic interpretation is that part of its SD
required to interpret it semantically. Since the semantic component requires only the sequence of underlying P-markers to
provide a sentence with its semantic interpretation, it follows
that a model of speech recognition need only assign to input sentences this much of their full SD.

The answer to the first of the two questions involves specifying
what syntactic information a model of speech recognition must
obtain from the phonetic representation of an input sentence to
arrive at the sequence of underlying P-markers. Here it seems
plausible that the recognition model should take advantage of the
fact that in our conception of the syntactic component each sentence has associated with it a single final derived P-marker,
which is the input to the phonological component and which is
hence that aspect of syntactic structure most closely related to
the phonetic shape of sentences. The most reasonable assumption is that the model of speech recognition must obtain from the
phonetic representation of an input utterance the final derived P-
marker associated with it by the syntactic component.

Hence, the following conception of a model of speech recognition emerges. The model has a component that operates on the
phonetic representation of the speech signal in order to find the

final derived P-marker of the sentence. This component employs the rules that are in both the syntactic and phonological components and most crucially relies on that part of the syntactic component which assigns constituent characterizations to morphemes. Moreover, the model has a component that operates on the output of this initial subcomponent to determine the sequences of underlying P-markers for the original input sentence. The first component would synthesize a set of final derived P-markers for strings of formatives equal in length to the input string, and when it found a match in this set, it would assign the final derived P-marker of the matching string to the input string. The second subcomponent is a function whose arguments are a final derived P-marker and a set of rules from the syntactic component, and whose values are sequences of underlying P-markers. However, it is somewhat unlikely that this function is an analysis-by-synthesis procedure because such a procedure introduces a certain lack of economy even with heuristics. It is an inherent feature of analysis by synthesis to provide an analysis by deriving not only the final structure but all intermediate structures as well. However, the second subcomponent of a recognition model, in so far as possible, should not attempt to specify the intermediate structures of a sentence that are assigned in the syntactic component — i.e., all the derived P-markers except the final one, the transformations of the T-marker. In other words, if the sequence of underlying P-markers can be obtained from the final derived P-marker without depending on such intermediate structures, the model ought to be constructed in such a way as to avoid such dependence.

The results of this monograph also have implications for the formulation of a model of speech production. The process of producing an utterance can be conceived of as starting with a message to be communicated in the form of a set of readings for some 'Sentence' node. The process follows a series of encoding steps, finally resulting in a phonetic representation of an utterance which is input to the physiological speech mechanism.

Thus, whereas the model of speech recognition takes an utterance as input and gives a set of readings as output, the model of speech production reverses the process, taking a set of readings as input and giving an utterance as output. With this conception of a speech production model, the fundamental question is: By what principles does the encoding work? More precisely, given a set of readings, how does the model select a set of sequences of underlying P-markers, each of which has this set of readings assigned to the 'Sentence' node of its leftmost member, and how does the model then choose that sequence from this set which underlies the final derived P-marker on which the phonological component operates to give the phonetic representation?

It is natural to think of a model of speech production as having an initial component that produces the set of sequences of underlying P-markers for the given set of readings. This component may work on an analysis-by-synthesis basis, where the match is between the given set of readings and the set of readings for a synthesized sequence of underlying P-markers. But such a component would probably be extremely uneconomical.

The second component of the speech production model would have to be a set of criteria for choosing a sequence of underlying P-markers in such a way that the one chosen yields, by application of the rules of the syntactic component, a final derived P-marker suitable for communication. That is, the final derived P-marker must determine, by means of the phonological component, an utterance that is not too long or too complicated, etc.

The condition of adequacy on such a procedure requires that, given the input set of readings, the procedure selects a sequence of underlying P-markers whose semantic interpretation provides the 'Sentence' node of the leftmost underlying P-marker in the sequence with just the given set of readings. Once the set of underlying P-markers is selected, it would be most economical to have the model of speech production provide this set of P-markers as input to the linguistic description to have that system of rules produce a final derived P-marker and, by virtue of the phonological component, the phonetic representation of the final derived P-marker. This is possible, however, only if each sequence of underlying P-markers, together with the syntactic component, uniquely determines a final derived P-marker, i.e., only if each sequence of underlying P-markers is associated with a unique T-marker in the syntactic component. But, under the present conception of the syntactic component, this is not the case. Optional transformations, such as the one producing these syntactically distinct sentences,

(1) a. John looked up the blond
     b. John looked the blond up

lead to cases in which the same sequence of underlying P-markers is mapped into distinct final derived P-markers.

There are at least two ways to handle this situation. One is to regard the problem as beyond the scope of a model of speech production. The differences between the various sentences that result from distinct final derived P-markers with the same sequence of underlying P-markers are only of stylistic relevance, since these sentences are paraphrases of one another. Thus an arbitrary sequence of optional transformations is selected when the sequence of underlying P-markers is supplied to the syntactic component. In this way, the model of speech production has a unique, though in one respect arbitrary, output for each input.

Another way of handling this situation is to indicate somehow by an appropriate symbol in the sequence of underlying P-markers which of the optional singulary transformations in the syntactic component are to apply in the derivation of a final derived P-marker. Of course, under this interpretation the transformations now considered optional would become obligatory. This way of handling the problem effectively guarantees that the final derived P-marker for any sequence of underlying P-markers will be unique. But this method conflicts with the aim of eliminating all nonmeaningful elements from underlying P-markers. The symbols that determine which singulary transformations apply cannot be considered meaningful because the applications of different singulary transformations have no effect on meaning. However, as we have seen in the case of the passive, this aim apparently cannot be satisfied without exception anyway. Furthermore, this problem is not really serious since, as suggested in Chapter 4, it is necessary to revise the conception of the underlying or phrase structure component of the grammar to allow complex, feature representations for morphemes and other dictionary entries. In these terms, the markers of otherwise optional singulary transformations can be considered features of morpheme entries rather than morphemes. And such features are in general meaningless. However, we continue to discuss the question in terms of markers that are morphemes. If there is a special set of dummy morphemes — one for each otherwise optional singulary transformation — such that these dummy morphemes serve to indicate when singulary transformations are to be applied, there is still a question of how a sequence of underlying P-markers with a subset of morphemes from this set is chosen. That is, the question is what determines the choice of one subset of such dummy morphemes over another. The advantage of this way of handling the problem of the uniqueness of association between a sequence of underlying P-markers and a final derived P-marker is that the choice of singularly transformations becomes an operation of the model of speech production. One means by which the model of speech production can make this choice is to have it governed by the criterion which ensures that the output sentence be neither too syntactically complicated, nor too long, nor otherwise undesirable for communication. The plausibility of this suggestion derives from the fact that a sentence S_1, distinguished from another sentence S_2 only by the presence of some singulary transformation in its T-marker, in many cases differs from S_2 in being less syntactically complicated.

Whichever way of handling the stylistic singulary transformations is adopted, the ultimate phonetic representation of the final derived P-marker serves as the signal to the mechanism of speech which, in turn, produces the actual utterance.[9]

The whole discussion of models of speech recognition and speech production would be greatly simplified if given in terms of the new conception of the syntactic component, described in Section 3.7. According to this conception, the base subcomponent of the syntactic component generates a single complex object which is, in effect, a combination of the underlying P-markers of a sentoid, called a Generalized P-marker. These Generalized P-markers are the input to both the semantic component and the transformational subcomponent of the syntactic component, which would then contain only singulary transformations. Under this conception, the recognition model recovers such a Generalized P-marker from a final derived P-marker, and a production model chooses a Generalized P-marker which has for its 'Sentence' reading(s) all, and only, those in the set to be encoded.

5.5 Implications for the Theory of Language Learning

In his review of Skinner's Verbal Behavior,[10] Chomsky argued that the conditioning theory conception of learning cannot account for the basic facts about human language learning, and he proposed an alternative conception of a theory to explain how language are learned. He writes:

> "The child who learns a language has in some sense con-
> structed the grammar for himself on the basis of his observa-
> tion of sentences and nonsentences (i. e. , corrections by the
> verbal community). Study of the actual observed ability of a
> speaker to distinguish sentences from nonsentences, detect
> ambiguities, etc. , apparently forces us to the conclusion that
> this grammar is of an extremely complex and abstract char-
> acter, and that the young child has succeeded in carrying out
> what from the formal point of view, at least, seems to be a
> remarkable type of theory construction. Furthermore, this
> task is accomplished in a comparable way by all children.
> Any theory of learning must cope with these facts."[11]

Chomsky goes on to say: "The fact that all normal children ac-
quire essentially comparable grammars of great complexity with
remarkable rapidity suggests that human beings are somehow
especially designed to do this, with a ... 'hypothesis-formulating'
ability of unknown character and complexity."[12] Thus, according
to Chomsky, the trouble with the conditioning theory conception
of how a language is learned is that straightforward generalization
of the syntactic regularities in the small, heterogeneous corpus
of sentences and nonsentences to which the child is exposed cannot account for the basic fact that what is learned (on the basis of
this corpus) is a highly complex deductive theory capable of generating and structuring the infinitely many sentences of the language.

The facts about the nature of a linguistic description revealed in the course of this work provide further support for Chomsky's conception of language learning as a process of constructing a theory of the over-all structure of the language. We have shown that of the entire set of P-markers assigned to a sentence in the syntactic component only the sequence of underlying P-markers is operated on by the rules of the semantic component. Thus of the various P-markers provided by the syntactic component for a sentence only the ones which underlie all the others describe that aspect of the structure of the sentence upon which its meaning depends. The final derived P-marker of a sentence is the one describing that aspect of the structure of the sentence which determines its realization in sound. Furthermore, it follows from our earlier discussions that, in infinitely many cases of various types, the syntactic structure of a sentence which is represented by its final derived P-marker is radically different from that represented by its sequence of underlying P-markers. It is characteristic of these cases that the structure revealed by the sequence of underlying P-markers is far richer than the structure revealed by the final derived P-marker. Only the final derived P-marker, together with its phonetic interpretation, directly describes the observable features of an utterance — that is, the segmentation, bracketing, and labeling that represents the utterance's observable structure. Therefore, the conditioning theory conception of language learning must claim that inductive generalization found in the child's corpus of utterances proceeds by abstracting at best only those regularities described by the final derived P-markers. Only these regularities are, in any sense, observable. But no purely inductive abstraction of such observable regularities in the child's small, heterogeneous corpus can yield the very different and far richer structure of sentences that is revealed by their sequence of underlying P-markers — just as no purely inductive abstraction of observable regularities in the behavior of gases can yield the very different and far richer structure of the molecular phenomena underlying observable gas behavior. Purely inductive abstraction from observable properties of phonetic objects in the child's corpus cannot, in principle, explain how the child learns to understand the meaning of sentences, because many of the syntactic features on which the meaning of sentoids depends are nonexistent in final derived P-markers and thus are in no way physically marked in phonetic objects. Hence, there are no observable features to indicate how a child can obtain a semantic interpretation that depends on information about syntactic properties not represented in final derived P-markers. But without such observable aspects of sentence structure from which to abstract, a conditioning theory has no basis for an abstraction that accounts for the way one relates semantic interpretations to

phonetic objects. For any conditioning theory — by definition —
presupposes observable aspects of a stimulus (in this case, aspects of sentence structure) to which something else (in this case,
semantic features, however construed) is conditioned. Therefore,
since no account of how children learn the meaning of sentences
is possible without the formulation of this richer structure found
in underlying P-markers, a conditioning theory of language acqui-
sition must be rejected as being, in principle, incapable of explaining how language is learned.

NOTES

1. There are, of course, mixed cases in which such a trans-
    formational relation combines with synonymity to produce
    a paraphrase relation.

2. For a survey of such arguments, cf., for example, Postal
    (1964), especially Chapter 6.

3. Cf. Postal (1964).

4. Cf. the discussion in note 18 of Chapter 3 and the following
    references: Halle (1959, 1962); Chomsky (1963, 1964 b);
    Halle and Chomsky (in preparation).

5. For support of this statement, cf. Halle (1959, 1962);
    Chomsky (1963, 1964 b); Halle and Chomsky (in prepa-
    ration).

6. For a description of morpheme structure rules, cf. Halle
    (1959); for a description of universal phonological rules in
    detail, cf. Postal (in preparation b).

7. There is a good chance of characterizing the modifier con-
    stituent in terms of the fact that it was optionally chosen in
    its rule of introduction. Cf. Lees (1961) for a discussion,
    which must, however, be extended for adequacy.

8. Matthews (1961); Halle and Stevens (1959); Herzberger (in
    preparation).

9. For further discussion of models of the speaker and hearer,
    cf. Chomsky and Miller (1963).

10. Chomsky (1959 b).

11. Ibid.

12. Ibid.

BIBLIOGRAPHY

Chomsky, N. (1955 a). The Logical Structure of Linguistic Theory, mimeographed, and microfilmed, M.I.T. Library, Cambridge, Mass.

——— (1955 b). Semantic Considerations in Grammar, The Institute of Languages and Linguistics, Monograph No. 8, pp. 141-153. Georgetown University, Washington, D.C.

——— (1957). Syntactic Structures. Mouton & Co., The Hague, The Netherlands.

——— (1959 a). "On Certain Formal Properties of Grammars," Information and Control, 2, pp. 137-167.

——— (1959 b). Review of Verbal Behavior, Language, 35.1, pp. 26-58.

——— (1961). "On the Notion 'Rule of Grammar'," Proceedings of the Symposium on the Structure of Language and Its Mathematical Aspects, American Mathematical Society, Vol. XII, pp. 6-24.

——— (1962). "A Transformational Approach to Syntax," Proceedings of the 3rd Texas Conference on Problems of Linguistic Analysis in English, pp. 124-158. University of Texas, Austin, Texas.

——— (1963 a). "Explanatory Models in Linguistics," Proceedings of the 1960 International Congress on Logic, Methodology and Philosophy of Science, E. Nagel, P. Suppes, and A. Tarski, editors, pp. 528-550. Stanford University Press, Stanford, Calif.

——— (1963 b). "Formal Properties of Grammars," Handbook of Mathematical Psychology, Vol. 2, Chap. 12, R. D. Luce, R. D. Bush, and E. Galanter, editors. John Wiley & Sons, New York, N.Y.

——— (1964 a). "Degrees of Grammaticalness," The Structure of Language: Readings in the Philosophy of Language, J. A. Fodor and J. J. Katz, editors. Prentice-Hall, Inc., Englewood Cliffs, N.J.

——— (1964 b). "Current Issues in Linguistic Theory," The Structure of Language: Readings in the Philosophy of Language, J. A. Fodor and J. J. Katz, editors. Prentice-Hall, Inc., Englewood Cliffs, N.J.

Chomsky, N., and Halle, M. (in preparation). The Sound Pattern of English.

—— and Miller, G. A. (1963). "Finitary Models of Language Users," in Handbook of Mathematical Psychology, Vol. 2, Chap. 13, R. D. Luce, R. D. Bush, and E. Galanter, editors. John Wiley & Sons, New York, N.Y.

Collingwood, R. G. (1940). An Essay on Metaphysics. Clarendon Press, Oxford, England.

Dixon, R. M. W. (1963). Linguistic Science and Logic, Mouton & Co., The Hague, The Netherlands.

Fillmore, C. J. (1962). Indirect Object Constructions in English and the Ordering of Transformations. Ohio State University, Project on Syntactic Analysis, Report No. 1, Columbus, Ohio.

—— (1963). "The Position of Embedding Transformations in a Grammar," Word, 19.2, pp. 208-231.

Goodenough, W. H. (1951). Property, Kin, and Community on Truk. Yale University Publications in Anthropology, No. 46, New Haven, Conn.

—— (1956). "Componential Analysis and the Study of Meaning," Language, 32.1, pp. 195-216.

Halle, M. (1959). The Sound Pattern of Russian. Mouton & Co., The Hague, Netherlands.

—— (1962). "Phonology and Generative Grammar," Word, 18, pp. 54-72.

—— and Stevens, K. (1959). "Analysis by Synthesis," Proceedings of the Seminar on Speech Compression and Processing, L. E. Woods and W. Wathen-Dunn, editors, AFCRC-TR-'59-198, Vol. II, Paper D7.

Herzberger, H. (in preparation). "A Decision Procedure for Grammars," mimeographed.

Hockett, C. F. (1961). "Linguistic Elements and Their Relations," Language, 37.1, pp. 29-53.

Katz, J. J. (1964 a). "Semi-sentences," The Structure of Language: Readings in the Philosophy of Language, J. A. Fodor and J. J. Katz, editors. Prentice-Hall, Inc., Englewood Cliffs, N.J.

—— (1964 b). "Analyticity and Contradiction in Natural Language," The Structure of Language: Readings in the Philosophy of Language, J. A. Fodor and J. J. Katz, editors. Prentice-Hall, Inc., Englewood Cliffs, N.J.

—— and Fodor, J. A. (1963). "The Structure of a Semantic Theory," Language, 39, pp. 170-210.

Klima, E. (1962). "Relatedness between Grammatical Systems," Quarterly Progress Report, No. 65, Research Laboratory of Electronics, M.I.T., Cambridge, Mass.

—— (1964). "Negation in English," The Structure of Language: Readings in the Philosophy of Language, J. A. Fodor and J. J. Katz, editors. Prentice-Hall, Inc., Englewood Cliffs, N.J.

Lees, R. B. (1960). The Grammar of English Nominalizations, Supplement to International Journal of American Linguistics, 26.

—— (1961). "The Grammatical Basis of Some Semantic Notions," Proceedings of the 11th Annual Round Table Conference, The Institute of Languages and Linguistics, Monograph No. 11, pp. 5-20. Georgetown University, Washington, D.C.

Lounsbury, F. G. (1956). "A Semantic Analysis of Pawnee Kinship Usage," Language, 32.1, pp. 158-194.

Matthews, G. H. (1961). "Analysis by Synthesis of Sentences of Natural Languages," Proceedings of the International Conference on Mechanical Translation and Applied Linguistics, National Physical Laboratory, Teddington, England.

Postal, P. (1964). "Constituent Structure," International Journal of American Linguistics, Publication 30 of Indiana University Research Center in Anthropology, Folklore, and Linguistics, Bloomington, Ind.

—— (in preparation a). "Questions in English."

—— (in preparation b). Mohawk Phonology.

Quine, W. V. (1953). "Two Dogmas of Empiricism," From a Logical Point of View. Havard University Press, Cambridge, Mass.

Stockwell, R. P. (1960). "The Place of Intonation in a Generative Grammar of English," Language, 36.3, pp. 360-367.

Strawson, P. F. (1956). "On Referring," Essays in Conceptual Analysis, A. Flew, editor, pp. 21-52. The Macmillan Company, New York, N.Y.

Wallace, A. F. C., and Atkins, J. (1960). "The Meaning of
  Kinship Terms," American Anthropologist, 62.1, pp. 58-80.
  Menasha, Wisc.

Weinreich, U. (1963). "On the Semantic Structure of Language,"
  Universals of Language, J. H. Greenberg, editor. The M.I.T.
  Press, Cambridge, Mass.